The Complete

Junior Congregation

Synagogue Companion

THE COMPLETE JUNIOR CONGREGATION SYNAGOGUE COMPANION

FIRST EDITION
Copyright ©2004
The Jewish Learning Group, Inc.

Published by

the JEWISH
LEARNING GROUP

Tel. 1-(888)-56-LEARN
www.JewishLearningGroup.com
Email: info@JewishLearningGroup.com

ISBN 1-891293-19-2

Acknowledgements

To Rabbi Sholom Ber Chaikin, for giving selflessly of his valuable time to read, amend, and refine the material presented here, and for ensuring its Halachic accuracy.

To Rabbi Gavriel Zinner, for clarifying various Halachic questions. To Rabbi Shmuel Rabin for expertly proofing the Hebrew text of the prayers and blessings.

To the countless rabbis and lay-leaders who have offered their creative ideas, advice, and never-ending encouragement.

And to everyone else who helped make this book possible!

We have devised the following transliteration system to help readers accurately pronounce the Hebrew words of blessings and prayers presented in this book.

Hebrew:	Transliteration:	Example:
כ or ח	ch	Challah
ָ	ö	Law
ַ	a	Hurrah
ֵ	ay	Today
ֶ	e	Leg
ְ	'	Avid
ֹ or וֹ	o	Tone
ִ	i	Key
ֻ or וּ	u	Lunar
יַ	ai	Aisle
יָ	öy	Toy

Table of Contents

How To Use This Book

All the basic prayers of the Friday night and Shabbat morning services are included, along with brief instructions and explanations. Often, the full translations of prayers have been abbreviated or replaced with descriptive text to aid in comprehension.

In order to address the wide range of age groups and knowledge levels of those using this Companion, we have instituted a simplified system for selecting prayers. All prayers are marked following three groupings: Early beginners, intermediate, and advanced. The groups also reflect ages 2-4, 5-7, 8-10. Each prayer section has been marked for one or all of these three groups. This approach ensures that the earliest beginners will at least recite the minimally required prayers, as well as provide a gradually ascending training program, so that one may soon pray out of a regular "Siddur," (prayer book).

Directions: At the beginning of each prayer, look for the level you decided to follow. If your level is listed, recite the prayer. If not, then you may choose to skip the prayer and proceed to the following prayer.

Please note: The selection and organization of prayers in this book is for educational purposes only. One is not limited to the listed prayers, but may add or substitute prayers found here or in a complete Siddur, each according to their level.

The Junior Congregation Synagogue Companion

Level Ⓐ	Level Ⓑ	Level Ⓒ
Early Beginners	Intermediate	Advanced

• Friday Night •

Lecho Dodi (first), 23	Yedid Nefesh, 15	Yedid Nefesh, 15
Shema/Veohavto, 32	Mizmor Ledovid, 21	Lechu Neraneno, 17
Tzorchai Am'cho, 158	Lecho Dodi, 23	Shiru Lashem, 19
Torah Tzivoh, 144	Maariv Arovim, 29	Mizmor Ledovid, 21
Al Tiro, 141	Shema/Veohavto, 32	Lecho Dodi, 23
	Vehoyo/Vayomer, 34	Mikolos Mayim, 28
	Mi Chomocho, 39	Maariv Arovim, 29
	Amidah (parts), 40	Ahavas Olom, 30
	Vayechulu, 56	Shema/Veohavto, 32
	Mogayn Ovos, 57	Vehoyo/Vayomer, 34
	Olaynu, 59	Mi Chomocho, 39
	Al Tiro, 62	Amidah, 40
		Vayechulu, 56
		Mogayn Ovos, 57
		Olaynu, 59
		V'al Kayn, 60
		Al Tiro, 62

• Shabbat Day •

Modeh Ani/Netilas, 64	Modeh Ani/Netilas, 64	Modeh Ani/Netilas, 64
Birkas Hatorah, 76	Asher Yotzar/Brochos, 66	Asher Yotzar/Brochos, 66
Birkas Tzitzis, 79	Birkas Hatorah, 75	Birkas Hatorah, 75
Haraini M'kabel, 80	Birkas Tzitzis, 79	Birkas Tzitzis, 79

7

The Junior Congregation Synagogue Companion

Level A	Level B	Level C
Early Beginners	**Intermediate**	**Advanced**
Ma Tovu, 80	Haraini M'kabel, 80	Haraini M'kabel, 80
Ashrei (first few lines), 88	Ma Tovu/Adon Olom, 80	Ma Tovu/Adon Olom, 80
Shema/Veohavto, 100	Boruch Sheomar, 85	Hoaderes, 83
Tzorchai Am'cho, 158	Ashrei, 88	Boruch Sheomar, 85
Al Tiro, 141	Yishtabach, 93	Ashrei, 88
The 12 Pesukim, 144	Yotzayr Or, 95	Halelukoh B'kodsho, 91
	Kel Odon, 95	Boruch Hashem Leolom, 92
	Shema/Veohavto, 100	Yishtabach, 93
	Vehoyo/Vayomer, 102	Yotzayr Or, 95
	Shiro Chadosho, 108	Kel Odon, 95
	Amidah (parts), 109	Es Shaim, 97
	Kedusha/Modim, 113,121	Lokel Boruch, 98
	Vayehi Binsoa/V'zos, 129	Shema/Veohavto, 100
	Musof Amidah (parts), 131	Vehoyo/Vayomer, 102
	Kedusha/Modim, 134,135	Veyatziv, 107
	Ain Kelokainu, 136	Shiro Chadosho, 108
	Olaynu, 137	Amidah, 109
	Al Tiro, 141	Kedusha/Modim, 113,121
	Tehilim - Chapter 20, 142	Vayehi Binsoa/V'zos, 129
	The 12 Pesukim, 144	Birkas Hachodesh, 130
		Musof/Kedusha/Modim, 131
		Ain Kelokainu, 136
		Olaynu, 137
		V'al Kayn/Al Tiro, 139
		Tehilim - Chapter 20, 142
		The 12 Pesukim, 144

The Junior Congregation Synagogue Companion

א	בּ	בּ	ג	ד	ה	ו
Alef	Beis	Veis	Gimmel	Daled	Hey	Vöv

ז	ח	ט	י	כּ	כ	ך
Zayin	Ches	Tes	Yud	Köf	Chöf	Long Chöf

ל	מ	ם	נ	ן	ס	ע
Lamed	Mem	Closed Mem	Nun	Long Nun	Samech	Ayin

פּ	פ	ף	צ	ץ	ק	ר
Pey	Fey	Long Fey	Tzadik	Long Tzadik	Kuf	Reish

שׁ	שׂ	תּ	ת
Shin	Sin	Tof	Sof

וֹ	ְ	ֶ	ֵ	ַ	ָ
Cholöm	Sh'vö	Segol	Tzayrey	Patöch	Kömatz

ֱ	ֲ	ֳ	וּ	ֻ	ִ
Chatöf Segol	Chatöf Patöch	Chatöf Kömatz	Shoorook	Koobootz	Cheerik

9

Blessings for Candle Lighting

The light of the Shabbat candles brings peace and harmony to the world. This most important mitzvah was given specifically to Jewish women and girls. Our matriarch Rivkah blessed the candles from the young age of three, instituting this custom for all Jewish girls for all time. It is this 3700-year-old tradition which Jewish women observe in welcoming the Shabbat, which rekindles the Divine spark in every Jewish being.

Light the candles, then spread your hands out around the candles, drawing your hands inward in a circular motion three times, to indicate the acceptance of the sanctity of Shabbat. Then cover your eyes and recite the appropriate blessing.

On Friday Evening

Böruch atöh adonöy,	בָּרוּךְ אַתָּה יְיָ,
elohaynu melech hö-olöm,	אֱלֹהֵינוּ מֶלֶךְ הָעוֹלָם,
asher kid'shönu b'mitzvosöv,	אֲשֶׁר קִדְּשָׁנוּ בְּמִצְוֹתָיו,
v'tzivönu l'hadlik nayr	וְצִוָּנוּ לְהַדְלִיק נֵר
shel shabös kodesh.	שֶׁל שַׁבָּת קֹדֶשׁ:

Blessed are You, God, King of the world, who has made us holy with His mitzvot, and commanded us to light the Shabbat candles.

On the Eve of Pesach, Shavuot and Sukkot

Böruch atöh adonöy,	בָּרוּךְ אַתָּה יְיָ,
elohaynu melech hö-olöm,	אֱלֹהֵינוּ מֶלֶךְ הָעוֹלָם,
asher kid'shönu b'mitzvosöv,	אֲשֶׁר קִדְּשָׁנוּ בְּמִצְוֹתָיו,
v'tzivönu l'hadlik nayr	וְצִוָּנוּ לְהַדְלִיק נֵר
shel yom tov.	שֶׁל יוֹם טוֹב:

Blessed are You, God, King of the world, who has made us holy with His mitzvot, and commanded us to light the holiday candles.

Continue with:
(Except on the last two nights of Passover)

Böruch atöh adonöy,	בָּרוּךְ אַתָּה יְיָ,
elohaynu melech hö-olöm,	אֱלֹהֵינוּ מֶלֶךְ הָעוֹלָם,
shehecheyönu v'kiy'mönu	שֶׁהֶחֱיָנוּ וְקִיְּמָנוּ
v'higi-önu liz'man ha-zeh.	וְהִגִּיעָנוּ לִזְמַן הַזֶּה:

Blessed are You, God, King of the world, who has enabled us to live to see this day.

11

On the Eve of Shabbat and Festivals

Böruch atöh adonöy,	בָּרוּךְ אַתָּה יְיָ,
elohaynu melech hö-olöm,	אֱלֹהֵינוּ מֶלֶךְ הָעוֹלָם,
asher kid'shönu b'mitzvosöv,	אֲשֶׁר קִדְּשָׁנוּ בְּמִצְוֹתָיו,
v'tzivönu l'hadlik nayr	וְצִוָּנוּ לְהַדְלִיק נֵר
shel shabös v'shel yom tov.	שֶׁל שַׁבָּת וְשֶׁל יוֹם טוֹב:

Blessed are You, God, King of the world, who has made us holy with His mitzvot, and commanded us to light the Shabbat and holiday candles.

Continue with:
(Except on the last two nights of Passover)

Böruch atöh adonöy,	בָּרוּךְ אַתָּה יְיָ,
elohaynu melech hö-olöm,	אֱלֹהֵינוּ מֶלֶךְ הָעוֹלָם,
shehecheyönu v'kiy'mönu	שֶׁהֶחֱיָנוּ וְקִיְּמָנוּ
v'higi-önu liz'man ha-zeh.	וְהִגִּיעָנוּ לִזְמַן הַזֶּה:

Blessed are You, God, King of the world, who has enabled us to live to see this day.

Why Do We Pray?

God commanded the Jewish people to pray to Him for their every need. He wants to hear from them and care for them, like a father and his own dear children. In fact, in the prayers we often address God as "our Father in heaven," for God regards us, and we regard ourselves, as His children.

In prayer we can, and should, ask God for anything we desire and wish for. God promised us that he will always listen to our prayers, even the prayers of a little child.

You may ask, why do we have to pray to God for our needs? Doesn't God know our needs even better than we do ourselves? Is not God, by His very nature, good and kind, and always willing to do us good? After all, children do not pray to their parents to feed them, and clothe them, and protect them; why should we pray to our Heavenly Father for such things?

It has been explained by our wise Sages that we are told to offer prayers to God in order to recognize the principle that God takes notice of our ways, that He can make them successful if we serve Him, or disastrous if we disobey Him; that success and failure are not the result of chance or accident.

13

It is important for us to acknowledge our dependence on God for our very life, our health, our daily bread, and our general welfare, for this is how it really is.

And so, we pray every day, and many times a day. We need to remind ourselves that our life and happiness are a gift from our Creator, and in turn we try to be worthy of God's kindnesses and favors to us.

Knowing that God is good and that nothing is impossible for Him to do, we go about our life with a deep sense of confidence and security. Even in times of pain and hardship we will not give up, knowing that in some way best known to God, whatever happens to us is for our own good.

We gain strength, courage and hope by trusting in God, and our daily prayers strengthen this trust in God. "In God We Trust" has been our Jewish motto since we first became a people.

On Shabbat, our prayers take on a different focus, as we turn our prayers to thank God for giving us the Shabbat Day and for choosing us to be His people. Indeed, on this day we "forget" about our worldly needs and matters, and instead ascend to a higher, more spiritual level, praising the Almighty God Who created the world in six days and rested on the seventh — the holy day of Shabbat.

The Friday Evening Service

Y'did Nefesh...

For Levels:
Ⓑ Ⓒ

יְדִיד נֶפֶשׁ...

Y'did nefesh öv höra-chamön,	יְדִיד נֶפֶשׁ אָב הָרַחֲמָן,
m'shoch av-d'chö el	מְשׁוֹךְ עַבְדְּךָ אֶל
r'tzonechö, yörutz av-d'chö	רְצוֹנֶךָ, יָרוּץ עַבְדְּךָ
k'mo ayöl, yishta-chaveh el	כְּמוֹ אַיָּל, יִשְׁתַּחֲוֶה אֶל
mul ha-dörechö, ye-erav lo	מוּל הֲדָרֶךָ, יֶעֱרַב לוֹ
y'dido-sechö, mi-no-fes tzuf	יְדִידוֹתֶיךָ, מִנּוֹפֶת צוּף
v'chöl tö-am.	וְכָל טָעַם.

Hödur nö-eh ziv hö-olöm,	הָדוּר נָאֶה זִיו הָעוֹלָם,
nafshi cholas ahavö-sechö,	נַפְשִׁי חוֹלַת אַהֲבָתֶךָ,
önö ayl nö r'fö nö löh,	אָנָּא אֵל נָא רְפָא נָא לָהּ,
b'har-os löh no-am zivechö,	בְּהַרְאוֹת לָהּ נוֹעַם זִיוֶךָ,

15

öz tis-chazayk v'sis-rapay,	אָז תִּתְחַזֵּק וְתִתְרַפֵּא,
v'hö-y'söh löh sim-chas olöm.	וְהָיְתָה לָהּ שִׂמְחַת עוֹלָם.

Vösik ye-hemu racha-mechö,	וָתִיק יֶהֱמוּ רַחֲמֶיךָ,
v'chusö nö al bayn ahu-vechö,	וְחוּסָה נָּא עַל בֵּן אֲהוּבֶךָ,
ki zeh kamöh nich-sof	כִּי זֶה כַּמָּה נִכְסוֹף
nich-safti lir-os b'sif-eres	נִכְסַפְתִּי לִרְאוֹת בְּתִפְאֶרֶת
uzechö, ay-leh chö-m'döh libi	עֻזֶּךָ, אֵלֶּה חָמְדָה לִבִּי
v'chusöh nö v'al tis-alöm.	וְחוּסָה נָּא וְאַל תִּתְעַלָּם.

Higö-leh nö uf'ros chavivi ölai	הִגָּלֶה נָא וּפְרוֹס חֲבִיבִי עָלַי
es sukas sh'lomechö, tö-ir	אֶת סֻכַּת שְׁלוֹמֶךָ, תָּאִיר
eretz mik'vodechö, nögilöh	אֶרֶץ מִכְּבוֹדֶךָ, נָגִילָה
v'nis-m'chöh böch, ma-hayr	וְנִשְׂמְחָה בָּךְ, מַהֵר
öhuv ki vö mo-ayd,	אָהוּב כִּי בָא מוֹעֵד,
v'chönaynu kimay olöm.	וְחָנֵּנוּ כִּימֵי עוֹלָם.

This prayer speaks of the longing of the Jewish soul for God, Creator of the World. We ask God to draw us close to Him and show us His kindness. We express our intense desire to serve Him out of our great love and desire for revealed Godliness.

16

Lechu N'ran'nah...

For Levels:

C

לְכוּ נְרַנְּנָה...

L'chu n'ran'nöh la-donöy,	לְכוּ נְרַנְּנָה לַיָי,
nöri-öh l'tzur yish-aynu.	נָרִיעָה לְצוּר יִשְׁעֵנוּ :
N'kad'möh fönöv b'sodöh,	נְקַדְּמָה פָנָיו בְּתוֹדָה,
biz'miros nöri-a lo.	בִּזְמִרוֹת נָרִיעַ לוֹ :
Ki ayl gödol adonöy, umelech	כִּי אֵל גָּדוֹל יְיָ, וּמֶלֶךְ
gödol al köl elohim. Asher	גָּדוֹל עַל כָּל אֱלֹהִים : אֲשֶׁר
b'yödo mech-k'ray öretz,	בְּיָדוֹ מֶחְקְרֵי אָרֶץ,
v'so-afos hörim lo.	וְתוֹעֲפוֹת הָרִים לוֹ :
Asher lo ha-yöm v'hu ösöhu,	אֲשֶׁר לוֹ הַיָּם וְהוּא עָשָׂהוּ,
v'yabeshes yödöv yö-tzöru.	וְיַבֶּשֶׁת יָדָיו יָצָרוּ :
Bo-u nish-tachaveh v'nichrö-öh,	בֹּאוּ נִשְׁתַּחֲוֶה וְנִכְרָעָה,
niv-r'chöh lif'nay adonöy	נִבְרְכָה לִפְנֵי יְיָ
osaynu. Ki hu elohaynu	עֹשֵׂנוּ : כִּי הוּא אֱלֹהֵינוּ
va-anachnu am mar-iso v'tzon	וַאֲנַחְנוּ עַם מַרְעִיתוֹ וְצֹאן

יָדוֹ, הַיּוֹם אִם בְּקֹלוֹ   yödo, ha-yom im b'kolo

תִשְׁמָעוּ: אַל תַּקְשׁוּ   sishmö-u. Al tak-shu

לְבַבְכֶם כִּמְרִיבָה, כְּיוֹם   l'vav'chem kim'rivöh, k'yom

מַסָּה בַּמִּדְבָּר: אֲשֶׁר נִסּוּנִי   masö ba-midbör. Asher nisuni

אֲבוֹתֵיכֶם, בְּחָנוּנִי, גַּם   avosaychem, b'chönuni, gam

רָאוּ פָעֳלִי: אַרְבָּעִים שָׁנָה   rö-u fö-öli. Arbö-im shönöh

אָקוּט בְּדוֹר, וָאֹמַר עַם תֹּעֵי   ökut b'dor, vö-omar am to-ay

לֵבָב הֵם וְהֵם לֹא יָדְעוּ   layvöv haym v'haym lo yöd'u

דְרָכָי: אֲשֶׁר נִשְׁבַּעְתִּי בְאַפִּי,   d'röchöy. Asher nishba-ti v'api,

אִם יְבֹאוּן אֶל מְנוּחָתִי: im y'vo-un el m'nuchösi.

In this Psalm we find the first created man, Adam's prayer after God breathed into him the Breath of Life: "Come, let us bow down before the Lord our Maker." He called to all creatures of the world to acknowledge the Creator and to submit to His will. The Psalm also notes the special relationship we have with God, how we are His people and He looks after us as a shepherd tends to his flock. It concludes with the miraculous exodus from Egypt, over 3,300 years ago, where God first showed His personal concern for our people.

Shiru La-shem...

For Levels:
6

שִׁירוּ לַיְיָ ...

Shiru la-donöy shir chödösh,	שִׁירוּ לַיְיָ שִׁיר חָדָשׁ,
shiru la-donöy köl hö-öretz.	שִׁירוּ לַיְיָ כָּל הָאָרֶץ:
Shiru ladonöy bö-r'chu sh'mo,	שִׁירוּ לַיְיָ בָּרְכוּ שְׁמוֹ,
bas'ru mi-yom l'yom y'shu-öso.	בַּשְּׂרוּ מִיּוֹם לְיוֹם יְשׁוּעָתוֹ:
Sap'ru vago-yim k'vodo, b'chöl	סַפְּרוּ בַגּוֹיִם כְּבוֹדוֹ, בְּכָל
hö-amim nif-l'osöv. Ki gödol	הָעַמִּים נִפְלְאוֹתָיו: כִּי גָדוֹל
adonöy um'hulöl m'od, norö	יְיָ וּמְהֻלָּל מְאֹד, נוֹרָא
hu al köl elohim. Ki köl	הוּא עַל כָּל אֱלֹהִים: כִּי כָּל
elohay hö-amim elilim,	אֱלֹהֵי הָעַמִּים אֱלִילִים,
vadonöy shöma-yim ösöh.	וַיְיָ שָׁמַיִם עָשָׂה:
Hod v'hödör l'fönöv, oz	הוֹד וְהָדָר לְפָנָיו, עֹז
v'sif-eres b'mik-dösho. Hövu	וְתִפְאֶרֶת בְּמִקְדָּשׁוֹ: הָבוּ
ladonöy mish-p'chos amim,	לַיְיָ מִשְׁפְּחוֹת עַמִּים,
hövu ladonöy kövod vö-oz.	הָבוּ לַיְיָ כָּבוֹד וָעֹז:

Hövu la-donöy k'vod	הָבוּ לַיְיָ כְּבוֹד
sh'mo, s'u min-chöh uvo-u	שְׁמוֹ, שְׂאוּ מִנְחָה וּבֹאוּ
l'chatz'rosöv. Hish-tachavu	לְחַצְרוֹתָיו: הִשְׁתַּחֲווּ
ladonöy b'had'ras kodesh, chilu	לַיְיָ בְּהַדְרַת קֹדֶשׁ,
mipönöv köl hö-öretz. Im'ru	חִילוּ מִפָּנָיו כָּל הָאָרֶץ:
vago-yim adonöy mölöch,	אִמְרוּ בַגּוֹיִם יְיָ מָלָךְ,
af tikon tayvayl bal timot,	אַף תִּכּוֹן תֵּבֵל בַּל תִּמּוֹט,
yödin amim b'mayshörim.	יָדִין עַמִּים בְּמֵישָׁרִים:
Yis-m'chu ha-shöma-yim	יִשְׂמְחוּ הַשָּׁמַיִם
v'sögayl hö-öretz, yir-am	וְתָגֵל הָאָרֶץ, יִרְעַם
hayöm um'lo-o. Ya-aloz södai	הַיָּם וּמְלֹאוֹ: יַעֲלֹז שָׂדַי
v'chöl asher bo, öz y'ran'nu köl	וְכָל אֲשֶׁר בּוֹ, אָז יְרַנְּנוּ כָּל
atzay yö-ar. Lif'nay adonöy ki	עֲצֵי יָעַר: לִפְנֵי יְיָ כִּי בָא, כִּי
vö, ki vö lishpot hö-öretz,	בָא לִשְׁפֹּט הָאָרֶץ,
yishpot tayvayl b'tzedek,	יִשְׁפֹּט תֵּבֵל בְּצֶדֶק,
v'amim be-emunöso.	וְעַמִּים בֶּאֱמוּנָתוֹ:

This Psalm too begins with a call to sing God's praises. It speaks of the Messianic era, when the extraordinary salvation that God will bring to our

20

people will call for a new kind of praise. The revelation of God's majesty in those future days will cause all mankind to worship God with a sense of holiness and awe.

Mizmor L'dövid...   **For Levels:**   מִזְמוֹר לְדָוִד...

𝓑 𝓒

Recited Standing

Mizmor l'dövid, hövu la-donöy	מִזְמוֹר לְדָוִד, הָבוּ לַיָי
b'nay aylim, hövu la-donöy	בְּנֵי אֵלִים, הָבוּ לַיָי
kövod vö-oz. Hövu la-donöy	כָּבוֹד וָעֹז: הָבוּ לַיָי
k'vod sh'mo, hishtachavu	כְּבוֹד שְׁמוֹ, הִשְׁתַּחֲווּ
la-donöy b'had'ras kodesh.	לַיָי בְּהַדְרַת קֹדֶשׁ:
Kol adonöy al ha-mö-yim,	קוֹל יְיָ עַל הַמָּיִם,
ayl ha-kövod hir-im, adonöy al	אֵל הַכָּבוֹד הִרְעִים, יְיָ עַל
ma-yim rabim. Kol adonöy	מַיִם רַבִּים: קוֹל יְיָ
bako-ach, kol adonöy be-hödör.	בַּכֹּחַ, קוֹל יְיָ בֶּהָדָר:
Kol adonöy shovayr arözim,	קוֹל יְיָ שֹׁבֵר אֲרָזִים,
va-y'shabayr adonöy es ar'zay	וַיְשַׁבֵּר יְיָ אֶת אַרְזֵי
ha-l'vönon. Va-yarkidaym k'mo	הַלְּבָנוֹן: וַיַּרְקִידֵם כְּמוֹ

21

aygel, l'vönon v'siryon k'mo	עֵגֶל, לְבָנוֹן וְשִׂרְיוֹן כְּמוֹ
ven r'aymim. Kol adonöy	בֶן רְאֵמִים: קוֹל יְיָ
cho-tzayv la-havos aysh.	חֹצֵב לַהֲבוֹת אֵשׁ:
Kol adonöy yöchil midbör,	קוֹל יְיָ יָחִיל מִדְבָּר,
yöchil adonöy midbar	יָחִיל יְיָ מִדְבַּר
ködaysh. Kol adonöy y'cholayl	קָדֵשׁ: קוֹל יְיָ יְחוֹלֵל
a-yölos va-yechesof y'öros,	אַיָּלוֹת וַיֶּחֱשֹׂף יְעָרוֹת,
uv'haychölo, kulo omayr	וּבְהֵיכָלוֹ, כֻּלּוֹ אֹמֵר
kövod. Adonöy la-mabul	כָּבוֹד: יְיָ לַמַּבּוּל
yöshöv, va-yayshev adonöy	יָשָׁב, וַיֵּשֶׁב יְיָ
melech l'olöm. Adonöy oz	מֶלֶךְ לְעוֹלָם: יְיָ עֹז
l'amo yitayn, adonöy y'vöraych	לְעַמּוֹ יִתֵּן, יְיָ יְבָרֵךְ
es amo va-shölom.	אֶת עַמּוֹ בַשָּׁלוֹם:

This Psalm contains God's name 18 times, which is significant since it is the same as the numerical value of the Hebrew word *Chai* (life). The seven repetitions of the words *Kol Hashem* (Voice of the Lord), in this Psalm correspond to the seven days of Creation, when everything was created by God's word. In the kabbalah (Jewish mysticism) we are taught that a far-reaching and tremendous effect takes place in the Upper worlds when this Psalm is recited with concentration and joy.

L'chöh Dodi ...

For Levels:
Ⓐ Ⓑ Ⓒ

לְכָה דוֹדִי ...

Recited Standing. Level Ⓐ recites only first paragraph.

L'chöh dodi lik'ras kalöh, לְכָה דוֹדִי לִקְרַאת כַּלָּה,
p'nay shabös n'kab'löh. פְּנֵי שַׁבָּת נְקַבְּלָה :

L'chöh dodi lik'ras kalöh, לְכָה דוֹדִי לִקְרַאת כַּלָּה,
p'nay shabös n'kab'löh. פְּנֵי שַׁבָּת נְקַבְּלָה :

This beautiful hymn welcomes the Shabbat Queen. The refrain of this hymn *Lecho Dodi* and, indeed, the entire motif of the hymn, in which the Shabbat is represented as a "Queen" whom we go out to welcome, is based on a Talmudic source, where we are told how two great Sages went out to welcome the Shabbat Queen in this fashion.

Shömor v'zöchor b'dibur שָׁמוֹר וְזָכוֹר בְּדִבּוּר
echöd, hishmi-önu ayl אֶחָד, הִשְׁמִיעָנוּ אֵל
ha-m'yuchöd, adonöy echöd הַמְיֻחָד, יְיָ אֶחָד
ush'mo echöd, l'shaym וּשְׁמוֹ אֶחָד, לְשֵׁם
ul'sif-eres v'lis'hilöh. וּלְתִפְאֶרֶת וְלִתְהִלָּה :

23

L'chöh dodi lik'ras kalöh,	לְכָה דוֹדִי לִקְרַאת כַּלָּה,
p'nay shabös n'kab'löh.	פְּנֵי שַׁבָּת נְקַבְּלָה :
Lik'ras shabös l'chu	לִקְרַאת שַׁבָּת לְכוּ
v'nayl'chöh, ki hi m'kor	וְנֵלְכָה, כִּי הִיא מְקוֹר
ha-b'röchöh, may-rosh	הַבְּרָכָה, מֵראשׁ
mikedem n'suchöh, sof	מִקֶּדֶם נְסוּכָה, סוֹף
ma-aseh b'ma-chashövöh	מַעֲשֶׂה בְּמַחֲשָׁבָה
t'chilöh.	תְּחִלָּה :
L'chöh dodi lik'ras kalöh,	לְכָה דוֹדִי לִקְרַאת כַּלָּה,
p'nay shabös n'kab'löh.	פְּנֵי שַׁבָּת נְקַבְּלָה :
Mikdash melech ir m'luchöh,	מִקְדַּשׁ מֶלֶךְ עִיר מְלוּכָה,
kumi tz'i mitoch ha-hafaychöh,	קוּמִי צְאִי מִתּוֹךְ הַהֲפֵכָה,
rav löch sheves b'aymek	רַב לָךְ שֶׁבֶת בְּעֵמֶק
ha-böchö, v'hu yachmol	הַבָּכָא, וְהוּא יַחֲמוֹל
öla-yich chemlöh.	עָלַיִךְ חֶמְלָה :
L'chöh dodi lik'ras kalöh,	לְכָה דוֹדִי לִקְרַאת כַּלָּה,
p'nay shabös n'kab'löh.	פְּנֵי שַׁבָּת נְקַבְּלָה :

24

Hisna-ari may-öför kumi,	הִתְנַעֲרִי מֵעָפָר קוּמִי,
liv'shi big'day sif-artaych ami,	לְבְשִׁי בִּגְדֵי תִפְאַרְתֵּךְ עַמִּי,
al yad ben yishai bays	עַל יַד בֶּן יִשַׁי בֵּית
ha-lachmi, kör'vöh el	הַלַּחְמִי, קָרְבָה אֶל
nafshi g'ölöh.	נַפְשִׁי גְאָלָהּ:

L'chöh dodi lik'ras kalöh,	לְכָה דוֹדִי לִקְרַאת כַּלָּה,
p'nay shabös n'kab'löh.	פְּנֵי שַׁבָּת נְקַבְּלָה:

His-or'ri his-or'ri,	הִתְעוֹרְרִי הִתְעוֹרְרִי,
ki vö oraych kumi ori,	כִּי בָא אוֹרֵךְ קוּמִי אוֹרִי,
u-ri u-ri shir da-bayri,	עוּרִי עוּרִי שִׁיר דַּבֵּרִי,
k'vod adonöy öla-yich niglöh.	כְּבוֹד יְיָ עָלַיִךְ נִגְלָה:

L'chöh dodi lik'ras kalöh,	לְכָה דוֹדִי לִקְרַאת כַּלָּה,
p'nay shabös n'kab'löh.	פְּנֵי שַׁבָּת נְקַבְּלָה:

Lo say-voshi v'lo siköl'mi,	לֹא תֵבוֹשִׁי וְלֹא תִכָּלְמִי,

mah tish-tochachi umah	מַה תִּשְׁתּוֹחֲחִי וּמַה
te-hemi, böch ye-chesu ani-yay	תֶּהֱמִי, בָּךְ יֶחֱסוּ עֲנִיֵּי עַמִּי,
ami, v'niv-n'söh hö-ir al tilöh.	וְנִבְנְתָה הָעִיר עַל תִּלָּהּ :

L'chöh dodi lik'ras kalöh,	לְכָה דוֹדִי לִקְרַאת כַּלָּה,
p'nay shabös n'kab'löh.	פְּנֵי שַׁבָּת נְקַבְּלָה :

V'höyu lim'shisöh sho-sö-yich,	וְהָיוּ לִמְשִׁסָּה שׁאסָיִךְ,
v'röchaku köl m'val'ö-yich,	וְרָחֲקוּ כָּל מְבַלְּעָיִךְ,
yösis öla-yich elohö-yich,	יָשִׂישׂ עָלַיִךְ אֱלֹהָיִךְ,
kim'sos chösön al kalöh.	כִּמְשׂוֹשׂ חָתָן עַל כַּלָּה :

L'chöh dodi lik'ras kalöh,	לְכָה דוֹדִי לִקְרַאת כַּלָּה,
p'nay shabös n'kab'löh.	פְּנֵי שַׁבָּת נְקַבְּלָה :

Yömin us'mol tifro-tzi,	יָמִין וּשְׂמֹאל תִּפְרוֹצִי,
v'es adonöy ta-ari-tzi,	וְאֶת יְיָ תַּעֲרִיצִי,
al yad ish ben par-tzi,	עַל יַד אִישׁ בֶּן פַּרְצִי,

26

v'nis-m'chöh v'nögilöh.   :וְנִשְׂמְחָה וְנָגִילָה

L'chöh dodi lik'ras kalöh,   ,לְכָה דוֹדִי לִקְרַאת כַּלָּה
p'nay shabös n'kab'löh.   :פְּנֵי שַׁבָּת נְקַבְּלָה

Turn around, facing west, and say:

Bo-i v'shölom ateres ba-löh,   ,בּוֹאִי בְשָׁלוֹם עֲטֶרֶת בַּעְלָהּ

gam b'rinöh *(On Festivals substitute:*   גַּם בְּרִנָּה (ביו״ט: בְּשִׂמְחָה)

b'simchöh) uv'tzöhöloh, toch   וּבְצָהֳלָה, תּוֹךְ אֱמוּנֵי

emunay am s'gulöh, *(Bow right)*   ,עַם סְגֻלָּה, בּוֹאִי כַלָּה

bo-i chalöh, *(Bow left)* bo-i   בּוֹאִי כַלָּה, (ויאמר בלחש

chalöh, *(Say silently a third time:)*   פעם שלישית) בּוֹאִי כַלָּה

bo-i chalöh shabös mal-k'sö.   :שַׁבָּת מַלְכְּתָא

Turn back, facing east, bow forward, and say:

L'chöh dodi lik'ras kalöh,   ,לְכָה דוֹדִי לִקְרַאת כַּלָּה
p'nay shabös n'kab'löh.   :פְּנֵי שַׁבָּת נְקַבְּלָה

27

Adonöy Möloch...   **For Levels:**   יְיָ מָלָךְ...
6

Adonöy möloch gay-us	יְיָ מָלָךְ גֵּאוּת
lö-vaysh, lö-vaysh adonöy, oz	לָבֵשׁ, לָבֵשׁ יְיָ, עֹז
his-azör, af tikon tay-vayl	הִתְאַזָּר, אַף תִּכּוֹן תֵּבֵל
bal timot. Nöchon kis-achö	בַּל תִּמּוֹט: נָכוֹן כִּסְאֲךָ
may-öz, may-olöm ötöh.	מֵאָז, מֵעוֹלָם אָתָּה:
Nös'u n'höros adonöy, nös'u	נָשְׂאוּ נְהָרוֹת יְיָ, נָשְׂאוּ
n'höros kolöm, yis'u n'höros	נְהָרוֹת קוֹלָם, יִשְׂאוּ נְהָרוֹת
döch-yöm. Mikolos ma-yim	דָּכְיָם: מִקֹּלוֹת מַיִם
rabim adirim mishb'ray yöm,	רַבִּים אַדִּירִים מִשְׁבְּרֵי יָם,
adir ba-mörom adonöy.	אַדִּיר בַּמָּרוֹם יְיָ:
Aydo-sechö ne-em'nu m'od,	עֵדֹתֶיךָ נֶאֶמְנוּ מְאֹד,
l'vays'chö nö-avöh kodesh,	לְבֵיתְךָ נָאֲוָה קֹדֶשׁ,
adonöy, l'orech yömim.	יְיָ, לְאֹרֶךְ יָמִים:

This Psalm expresses the theme of God's rulership and strength.

28

The Leader says: ‏חזן :‏

Bör'chu es adonöy ‏בָּרְכוּ אֶת יְיָ‏
ha-m'voröch. ‏הַמְבֹרָךְ :‏

Congregation, then leader: ‏קהל וחזן :‏

Böruch adonöy ha-m'voröch ‏בָּרוּךְ יְיָ הַמְבֹרָךְ‏
l'olöm vö-ed. ‏לְעוֹלָם וָעֶד :‏

Ma-ariv Arövim... **For Levels:** ‏מַעֲרִיב עֲרָבִים...‏
Ⓑ Ⓒ

Böruch atöh adonöy elohaynu ‏בָּרוּךְ אַתָּה יְיָ אֱלֹהֵינוּ‏
melech hö-olöm, asher ‏מֶלֶךְ הָעוֹלָם, אֲשֶׁר‏
bid'vöro ma-ariv arövim, ‏בִּדְבָרוֹ מַעֲרִיב עֲרָבִים,‏
b'chöchmöh posay-ach sh'örim, ‏בְּחָכְמָה פּוֹתֵחַ שְׁעָרִים,‏
uvis'vunöh m'sha-neh itim, ‏וּבִתְבוּנָה מְשַׁנֶּה עִתִּים,‏
uma-chalif es ha-z'manim, ‏וּמַחֲלִיף אֶת הַזְּמַנִּים,‏
um'sader es ha-kochövim, ‏וּמְסַדֵּר אֶת הַכּוֹכָבִים,‏
b'mish-m'rosay-hem böröki-ah, ‏בְּמִשְׁמְרוֹתֵיהֶם בָּרָקִיעַ,‏

kir'tzono. Boray yom völöy-löh, כִּרְצוֹנוֹ. בּוֹרֵא יוֹם וָלָיְלָה,

go-layl or mip'nay cho-shech, גּוֹלֵל אוֹר מִפְּנֵי חֹשֶׁךְ,

v'cho-shech mip'nay or, וְחֹשֶׁךְ מִפְּנֵי אוֹר,

uma-avir yom umay-vi löy-löh, וּמַעֲבִיר יוֹם וּמֵבִיא לָיְלָה,

umavdil bayn yom uvayn וּמַבְדִּיל בֵּין יוֹם וּבֵין

löy-löh, adonöy tzvö-os sh'mo. לָיְלָה, יְיָ צְבָאוֹת שְׁמוֹ.

Böruch atöh adonöy, בָּרוּךְ אַתָּה יְיָ,

ha-ma-ariv arövim. הַמַּעֲרִיב עֲרָבִים:

With this blessing we acknowledge the awesome change from day to night. The opening verse refers to the first evening which God created, as it is written in Genesis, "And it was evening, and it was morning, one day." What may seem a 'natural' and 'ordinary' change from day to night, from night to day, from summer to winter, from winter to summer, and so on, is really a wonderful continuous act of Creation by God, not something to be taken for granted.

Ahavas Olöm...   **For Levels:**   אַהֲבַת עוֹלָם ...
𝟞

Ahavas olöm bays yisrö-ayl אַהֲבַת עוֹלָם בֵּית יִשְׂרָאֵל

am'chö öhöv'tö, toröh עַמְּךָ אָהָבְתָּ, תּוֹרָה

umitzvos, chukim umishpötim	וּמִצְוֹת, חֻקִּים וּמִשְׁפָּטִים
osönu li-mad-tö. Al kayn	אוֹתָנוּ לִמַּדְתָּ. עַל כֵּן
adonöy elo-haynu,	יְיָ אֱלֹהֵינוּ,
b'shöch'vaynu uv'kumaynu	בְּשָׁכְבֵנוּ וּבְקוּמֵנוּ
nösi-ach b'chu-kechö,	נָשִׂיחַ בְּחֻקֶּיךָ,
v'nismach b'div'ray so-rös'chö	וְנִשְׂמַח בְּדִבְרֵי תוֹרָתֶךָ
uv'mitzvosechö l'olöm vö-ed.	וּבְמִצְוֹתֶיךָ לְעוֹלָם וָעֶד.
Ki haym cha-yaynu	כִּי הֵם חַיֵּינוּ
v'orech yö-maynu, uvöhem	וְאֹרֶךְ יָמֵינוּ, וּבָהֶם
neh-ge yomöm vö-löy'löh.	נֶהְגֶּה יוֹמָם וָלָיְלָה,
V'a-havös'chö lo sösur mimenu	וְאַהֲבָתְךָ לֹא תָסוּר מִמֶּנּוּ
l'olömim. Böruch atöh adonoy,	לְעוֹלָמִים. בָּרוּךְ אַתָּה יְיָ,
ohayv amo yisrö-ayl.	אוֹהֵב עַמּוֹ יִשְׂרָאֵל:

This blessing is a fitting introduction to the Shema. It speaks of God's love for us, His people, and reminds us that the Torah and Mitzvot are not merely additions to our life, but our very life and only cause for existence.

Sh'ma Yisrö-ayl...   **For Levels:**   שְׁמַע יִשְׂרָאֵל...
𝒜 ℬ 𝒞

The *Shema* is the essence of our faith. It consists of three paragraphs taken from the Torah (Bible). The first paragraph begins with the statement: "The Lord is One." It goes on to tell us that we must love God and dedicate our lives to carrying out His will. This section also contains the two mitzvot of Tefillin and Mezuzah, which remind us that we are Jews.

The second chapter contains a promise that if we fulfill and observe God's commands we shall be a happy people in our land. If not, we will suffer exile and hardships in strange lands, so that by suffering and trouble we will learn the ways of God and return to Him.

The third chapter contains the commandment of Tzitzit, the distinctive Jewish garment which is a constant reminder of all the precepts of the Torah. We are reminded, also, that God brought us out of Egypt and made us His people, and that we accepted Him as our God.

It is customary to cover the eyes with our right hand while reciting the first verse of the *Shema*, to increase concentration.

Sh'ma yisrö-ayl, adonöy   שְׁמַע יִשְׂרָאֵל, יְיָ

elohaynu, adonöy echöd.   אֱלֹהֵינוּ, יְיָ אֶחָד:

Hear, O Israel, the Lord is our God, the Lord is One.

Remove your hand from your eyes, and say the following in an undertone:

Böruch shaym k'vod   בָּרוּךְ שֵׁם כְּבוֹד

mal'chuso l'olöm vö-ed.   מַלְכוּתוֹ לְעוֹלָם וָעֶד :

Blessed be the name of the glory of His kingdom forever and ever.

Continue in a regular tone below:

V'öhavtö ays adonöy elohechö,   וְאָהַבְתָּ אֵת יְיָ אֱלֹהֶיךָ,

b'chöl l'vöv'chö, uv'chöl   בְּכָל לְבָבְךָ, וּבְכָל

naf-sh'chö, uv'chöl m'odechö.   נַפְשְׁךָ, וּבְכָל מְאֹדֶךָ :

V'hö-yu ha-d'vörim hö-ay-leh   וְהָיוּ הַדְּבָרִים הָאֵלֶּה

asher önochi m'tzav'chö   אֲשֶׁר אָנֹכִי מְצַוְּךָ

ha-yom, al l'vö-vechö.   הַיּוֹם, עַל לְבָבֶךָ :

V'shinan-töm l'vö-nechö   וְשִׁנַּנְתָּם לְבָנֶיךָ

v'dibartö böm, b'shiv-t'chö   וְדִבַּרְתָּ בָּם, בְּשִׁבְתְּךָ

b'vaysechö, uv'lech-t'chö   בְּבֵיתֶךָ, וּבְלֶכְתְּךָ

vaderech, uv'shöch-b'chö,   בַדֶּרֶךְ, וּבְשָׁכְבְּךָ,

uv'kumechö. Uk'shartöm l'os   וּבְקוּמֶךָ : וּקְשַׁרְתָּם לְאוֹת

al yödechö, v'hö-yu l'totöfos   עַל יָדֶךָ, וְהָיוּ לְטֹטָפֹת

bayn aynechö. Uch'savtöm   בֵּין עֵינֶיךָ : וּכְתַבְתָּם

al m'zuzos bay-sechö, ‏עַל מְזֻזוֹת בֵּיתֶךָ,‏

uvish'örechö. ‏וּבִשְׁעָרֶיךָ:‏

You shall love the Lord your God with all your heart, with all your soul, and with all your might. And these words which I command you today shall be upon your heart. You shall teach them thoroughly to your children, and you shall speak of them when you sit in your house and when you walk on the road, when you lie down and when you rise. You shall bind them as a sign upon your hand, and they shall be for a reminder between your eyes. And you shall write them upon the doorposts of your house and upon your gates.

Levels ⑬ ⑥ continue below:

V'hö-yöh im shömo-a tish-m'u ‏וְהָיָה אִם שָׁמֹעַ תִּשְׁמְעוּ‏

el mitzvo-sai asher önochi ‏אֶל מִצְוֹתַי אֲשֶׁר אָנֹכִי‏

m'tza-veh es'chem ha-yom, ‏מְצַוֶּה אֶתְכֶם הַיּוֹם,‏

l'ahavöh es adonöy ‏לְאַהֲבָה אֶת יְיָ‏

elohaychem ul'öv'do, b'chöl ‏אֱלֹהֵיכֶם וּלְעָבְדוֹ, בְּכָל‏

l'vav'chem uv'chöl ‏לְבַבְכֶם וּבְכָל‏

naf-sh'chem. V'nösati m'tar ‏נַפְשְׁכֶם: וְנָתַתִּי מְטַר‏

artz'chem b'ito yo-reh ‏אַרְצְכֶם בְּעִתּוֹ יוֹרֶה‏

umalkosh, v'ösaftö d'gönechö ‏וּמַלְקוֹשׁ, וְאָסַפְתָּ דְגָנֶךָ‏

34

v'sirosh'chö v'yitz-hörechö.	וְתִירֹשְׁךָ וְיִצְהָרֶךָ׃
V'nösati aysev b'söd'chö	וְנָתַתִּי עֵשֶׂב בְּשָׂדְךָ
liv'hemtechö, v'öchaltö	לִבְהֶמְתֶּךָ, וְאָכַלְתָּ
v'sövö-tö. Hishöm'ru löchem	וְשָׂבָעְתָּ׃ הִשָּׁמְרוּ לָכֶם
pen yifteh l'vav'chem, v'sartem	פֶּן יִפְתֶּה לְבַבְכֶם, וְסַרְתֶּם
va-avad-tem elohim achayrim	וַעֲבַדְתֶּם אֱלֹהִים אֲחֵרִים
v'hish-tachavisem löhem.	וְהִשְׁתַּחֲוִיתֶם לָהֶם׃
V'chöröh af adonöy böchem	וְחָרָה אַף יְיָ בָּכֶם
v'ötzar es ha-shöma-yim v'lo	וְעָצַר אֶת הַשָּׁמַיִם וְלֹא
yih-yeh mötör v'hö-adömöh lo	יִהְיֶה מָטָר וְהָאֲדָמָה לֹא
sitayn es y'vulöh, va-avad-tem	תִתֵּן אֶת יְבוּלָהּ וַאֲבַדְתֶּם
m'hayröh may-al hö-öretz	מְהֵרָה מֵעַל הָאָרֶץ
ha-tovöh asher adonöy nosayn	הַטֹּבָה אֲשֶׁר יְיָ נֹתֵן
löchem. V'samtem es d'vörai	לָכֶם׃ וְשַׂמְתֶּם אֶת דְּבָרַי
ayleh al l'vav'chem v'al	אֵלֶּה עַל לְבַבְכֶם וְעַל
naf-sh'chem uk'shartem osöm	נַפְשְׁכֶם וּקְשַׁרְתֶּם אֹתָם
l'os al yed'chem v'hö-yu	לְאוֹת עַל יֶדְכֶם וְהָיוּ
l'totöfos bayn ay-naychem.	לְטוֹטָפֹת בֵּין עֵינֵיכֶם׃

V'limad-tem osöm es	וְלִמַּדְתֶּם אֹתָם אֶת
b'naychem l'dabayr böm,	בְּנֵיכֶם לְדַבֵּר בָּם,
b'shiv-t'chö b'vaysechö	בְּשִׁבְתְּךָ בְּבֵיתֶךָ
uv'lech-t'chö va-derech	וּבְלֶכְתְּךָ בַדֶּרֶךְ
uv'shöch-b'chö uv'kumechö.	וּבְשָׁכְבְּךָ וּבְקוּמֶךָ:
Uch'savtöm al m'zuzos	וּכְתַבְתָּם עַל מְזוּזוֹת
baysechö uvish'örechö.	בֵּיתֶךָ וּבִשְׁעָרֶיךָ:
L'ma-an yirbu y'maychem	לְמַעַן יִרְבּוּ יְמֵיכֶם
vimay v'naychem al	וִימֵי בְנֵיכֶם עַל
hö-adömöh asher nishba	הָאֲדָמָה אֲשֶׁר נִשְׁבַּע
adonöy la-avosaychem lösays	יְיָ לַאֲבֹתֵיכֶם לָתֵת
löhem, kimay ha-shöma-yim	לָהֶם, כִּימֵי הַשָּׁמַיִם
al hö-öretz.	עַל הָאָרֶץ:

And it will be, if you will diligently obey My commandments which I enjoin upon you this day, to love the Lord your God and to serve Him with all your heart and with all your soul, I will give rain for your land at the proper time, the early rain and the late rain, and you will gather in your grain, your wine and your oil. And I will give grass in your fields for your cattle, and you will eat and be sated. Take care lest your heart be lured away, and you turn astray and worship alien gods and bow down to them. For then the Lord's

36

wrath will flare up against you, and He will close the heavens so that there will be no rain and the earth will not yield its produce, and you will swiftly perish from the good land which the Lord gives you. Therefore, place these words of Mine upon your heart and upon your soul, and bind them for a sign on your hand, and they shall be for a reminder between your eyes. You shall teach them to your children, to speak of them when you sit in your house and when you walk on the road, when you lie down and when you rise. And you shall inscribe them on the doorposts of your house and on your gates – so that your days and the days of your children may be prolonged on the land which the Lord swore to your fathers to give to them for as long as the heavens are above the earth.

Va-yomer adonöy el mosheh	וַיֹּאמֶר יְיָ אֶל מֹשֶׁה
laymor. Dabayr el b'nay	לֵּאמֹר: דַּבֵּר אֶל בְּנֵי
yisrö-ayl v'ömartö alay-hem	יִשְׂרָאֵל וְאָמַרְתָּ אֲלֵהֶם
v'ösu löhem tzitzis al	וְעָשׂוּ לָהֶם צִיצִת עַל
kan'fay vig'dayhem l'dorosöm,	כַּנְפֵי בִגְדֵיהֶם לְדֹרֹתָם,
v'nös'nu al tzitzis ha-könöf,	וְנָתְנוּ עַל צִיצִת הַכָּנָף,
p'sil t'chayles. V'hö-yöh	פְּתִיל תְּכֵלֶת: וְהָיָה
löchem l'tzitzis, ur'isem oso	לָכֶם לְצִיצִת, וּרְאִיתֶם אֹתוֹ
uz'chartem es köl mitzvos	וּזְכַרְתֶּם אֶת כָּל מִצְוֹת
adonöy va-asisem osöm, v'lo	יְיָ וַעֲשִׂיתֶם אֹתָם, וְלֹא

37

sösuru acha-ray l'vav'chem	תָּתוּרוּ אַחֲרֵי לְבַבְכֶם
v'acharay aynay-chem asher	וְאַחֲרֵי עֵינֵיכֶם אֲשֶׁר
atem zonim acha-rayhem.	אַתֶּם זֹנִים אַחֲרֵיהֶם:
L'ma-an tiz-k'ru va-asisem es	לְמַעַן תִּזְכְּרוּ וַעֲשִׂיתֶם אֶת
köl mitzvo-söy, vih-yisem	כָּל מִצְוֹתָי, וִהְיִיתֶם
k'doshim laylo-haychem.	קְדֹשִׁים לֵאלֹהֵיכֶם:
Ani adonöy elo-haychem asher	אֲנִי יְיָ אֱלֹהֵיכֶם אֲשֶׁר
ho-tzaysi es'chem may-eretz	הוֹצֵאתִי אֶתְכֶם מֵאֶרֶץ
mitzra-yim lih-yos löchem	מִצְרַיִם לִהְיוֹת לָכֶם
laylohim, ani adonöy	לֵאלֹהִים, אֲנִי יְיָ
elo-haychem. Emes.	אֱלֹהֵיכֶם: אֱמֶת.

The Lord spoke to Moses, saying: Speak to the children of Israel and tell them to make for themselves fringes on the corners of their garments throughout their generations, and to attach a thread of blue on the fringe of each corner. They shall be to you as tzitzit, and you shall look upon them and remember all the commandments of the Lord and fulfill them, and you will not follow after your heart and after your eyes by which you go astray — so that you may remember and fulfill all My commandments and be holy to your God. I am the Lord your God who brought you out of the land of Egypt to be your God; I, the Lord, am your God. Truth...

Mi Chö-mochöh ...

For Levels:
B C

מִי כָמוֹכָה...

Mi chö-mochöh bö-aylim	מִי כָמֹכָה בָּאֵלִם
adonöy, mi kömochö ne-dör	יְיָ, מִי כָּמֹכָה נֶאְדָּר
ba-kodesh, norö s'hilos, osay	בַּקֹּדֶשׁ, נוֹרָא תְהִלֹּת, עֹשֵׂה
fe-le. Mal'chus'chö rö-u	פֶלֶא: מַלְכוּתְךָ רָאוּ
vönechö, bokay-a yöm lif'nay	בָנֶיךָ, בּוֹקֵעַ יָם לִפְנֵי
mosheh, zeh ayli önu v'öm'ru,	מֹשֶׁה, זֶה אֵלִי עָנוּ וְאָמְרוּ:
adonöy yimloch l'olöm vö-ed.	יְיָ יִמְלֹךְ לְעֹלָם וָעֶד.
V'ne-emar, ki födöh adonöy es	וְנֶאֱמַר: כִּי פָדָה יְיָ אֶת
ya-akov, ug'ölo mi-yad chözök	יַעֲקֹב, וּגְאָלוֹ מִיַּד חָזָק
mi-menu. Böruch atöh adonöy,	מִמֶּנּוּ. בָּרוּךְ אַתָּה יְיָ,
gö-al yisrö-ayl.	גָּאַל יִשְׂרָאֵל:

This prayer continues the themes of the preceding prayers. In it we proclaim the uniqueness of God, and make reference to the redemption that God has brought — and continues to bring — to the Jewish people.

The Amidah

For Levels:

ℬ 𝒞

עֲמִידָה

Recited standing, with feet together

[On Pesach, Shavuot, and Sukkot, a special Amidah is substituted, see Siddur]

Adonöy, s'fösai tif-töch ufi	אֲדֹנָי, שְׂפָתַי תִּפְתָּח וּפִי
yagid t'hilö-sechö.	יַגִּיד תְּהִלָּתֶךָ:

My Lord, open my lips, and my mouth shall declare Your praise.

Take three steps back, then three steps forward, as if approaching a king. At the word *Böruch* (blessed), bend the knee; at *Atöh* (You), bow forward; and at *Adonöy* (Lord), straighten up.

Böruch atöh adonöy elohaynu	בָּרוּךְ אַתָּה יְיָ אֱלֹהֵינוּ
vay-lohay avosaynu, elohay	וֵאלֹהֵי אֲבוֹתֵינוּ, אֱלֹהֵי
avröhöm, elohay yitzchök,	אַבְרָהָם, אֱלֹהֵי יִצְחָק,
vay-lohay ya-akov, hö-ayl	וֵאלֹהֵי יַעֲקֹב, הָאֵל
ha-gödol ha-gibor v'hanorö,	הַגָּדוֹל הַגִּבּוֹר וְהַנּוֹרָא,
ayl el-yon, gomayl chasödim	אֵל עֶלְיוֹן, גּוֹמֵל חֲסָדִים
tovim, konay ha-kol, v'zochayr	טוֹבִים, קוֹנֵה הַכֹּל, וְזוֹכֵר
chas'day övos, umayvi go-ayl	חַסְדֵי אָבוֹת, וּמֵבִיא גּוֹאֵל

livnay v'nayhem l'ma-an   לִבְנֵי בְנֵיהֶם לְמַעַן
sh'mo b'ahavöh.   שְׁמוֹ בְּאַהֲבָה:

Between Rosh Hashana and Yom Kippur add:

Zöch'raynu l'cha-yim,   זָכְרֵנוּ לְחַיִּים,
melech chöfaytz ba-cha-yim,   מֶלֶךְ חָפֵץ בַּחַיִּים,
v'chös'vaynu b'sayfer   וְכָתְבֵנוּ בְּסֵפֶר
ha-cha-yim, l'ma-an'chö   הַחַיִּים, לְמַעַנְךָ
elohim cha-yim.   אֱלֹהִים חַיִּים.

At the word *Böruch* (blessed), bend the knee; at *Atöh* (You), bow forward; and at *Adonöy* (Lord), straighten up.

Melech ozayr umoshi-a   מֶלֶךְ עוֹזֵר וּמוֹשִׁיעַ
umögayn. Böruch atöh   וּמָגֵן: בָּרוּךְ אַתָּה
adonöy, mögayn avröhöm.   יְיָ, מָגֵן אַבְרָהָם:

Blessed are You, Lord our God and God of our fathers, God of Abraham, God of Isaac and God of Jacob, the great, mighty and awesome God, exalted God, who bestows bountiful kindness, who creates all things, who remembers the piety of the Patriarchs, and who, in love, brings a redeemer to their children's children, for the sake of His Name. (*Between Rosh Hashana and Yom Kippur add*: Remember us for life, King who desires life; inscribe us in the Book of Life, for Your sake, O living God.) O King, [You are] a helper, a savior and a shield. Blessed are You Lord, Shield of Abraham.

41

Atöh gibor l'olöm adonöy,   אַתָּה גִבּוֹר לְעוֹלָם אֲדֹנָי,

m'cha-yeh maysim atöh,   מְחַיֶּה מֵתִים אַתָּה,

rav l'hoshi-a.   רַב לְהוֹשִׁיעַ:

In summer say: Morid ha-töl.   בַּקַּיִץ: מוֹרִיד הַטָּל:

In winter say: Mashiv höru-ach   בַּחוֹרֶף: מַשִּׁיב הָרוּחַ

umorid ha-geshem.   וּמוֹרִיד הַגֶּשֶׁם:

M'chalkayl cha-yim b'chesed,   מְכַלְכֵּל חַיִּים בְּחֶסֶד,

m'cha-yeh maysim b'rachamim   מְחַיֶּה מֵתִים בְּרַחֲמִים

rabim, somaych nof'lim,   רַבִּים, סוֹמֵךְ נוֹפְלִים,

v'rofay cholim, umatir   וְרוֹפֵא חוֹלִים, וּמַתִּיר

asurim, um'ka-yaym emunöso   אֲסוּרִים, וּמְקַיֵּם אֱמוּנָתוֹ

lishaynay öför, mi chömochö   לִישֵׁנֵי עָפָר, מִי כָמוֹךָ

ba-al g'vuros umi do-meh löch,   בַּעַל גְּבוּרוֹת וּמִי דוֹמֶה לָּךְ,

melech maymis um'cha-yeh   מֶלֶךְ מֵמִית וּמְחַיֶּה

umatzmi-ach y'shu-öh.   וּמַצְמִיחַ יְשׁוּעָה:

Mi chömochö öv hörachamön
zochayr y'tzuröv l'cha-yim
b'ra-chamim.

מִי כָמוֹךָ אַב הָרַחֲמָן
זוֹכֵר יְצוּרָיו לְחַיִּים
בְּרַחֲמִים:

V'ne-emön atöh l'ha-cha-yos
maysim. Boruch atöh adonöy,
m'cha-yeh ha-maysim.

וְנֶאֱמָן אַתָּה לְהַחֲיוֹת
מֵתִים. בָּרוּךְ אַתָּה יְיָ,
מְחַיֵּה הַמֵּתִים:

You are mighty forever, my Lord; You resurrect the dead; You are powerful to save. (*In summer say:* He causes the dew to descend.) (*In winter say:* He causes the wind to blow and the rain to fall.) He sustains the living with loving-kindness, resurrects the dead with great mercy, supports the falling, heals the sick, releases the bound, and fulfills His trust to those who sleep in the dust. Who is like You, mighty One! And who can be compared to You, King, who brings death and restores life, and causes deliverance to spring forth! (*Between Rosh Hashana and Yom Kippur add:* Who is like You, merciful Father, who in compassion remembers His creatures for life.) You are trustworthy to revive the dead. Blessed are You Lord, who revives the dead.

Atöh ködosh v'shim'chö
ködosh uk'doshim b'chöl yom
y'ha-l'luchö selöh. Boruch atöh
adonöy, hö-ayl ha-ködosh.

אַתָּה קָדוֹשׁ וְשִׁמְךָ
קָדוֹשׁ וּקְדוֹשִׁים בְּכָל יוֹם
יְהַלְלוּךָ סֶּלָה. בָּרוּךְ אַתָּה
יְיָ, הָאֵל הַקָּדוֹשׁ:

(*Between Rosh Hashana and Yom* **(בשבת שובה** :
Kippur substitute: Ha-melech ha-ködosh.) **הַמֶּלֶךְ הַקָּדוֹשׁ)**

You are holy and Your Name is holy, and holy beings praise You daily for all eternity. Blessed are You Lord, the holy God. (*Between Rosh Hashana and Yom Kippur substitute:* the holy King.)

Level 𝒢 continue below:

Atöh kidashtö es yom **אַתָּה קִדַּשְׁתָּ אֶת יוֹם**

ha-sh'vi-i lish'mechö, tachlis **הַשְּׁבִיעִי לִשְׁמֶךָ, תַּכְלִית**

ma-asay shöma-yim vö-öretz, **מַעֲשֵׂה שָׁמַיִם וָאָרֶץ,**

bay-rachto miköl ha-yömim, **בֵּרַכְתּוֹ מִכָּל הַיָּמִים,**

v'kidashto miköl ha-z'manim, **וְקִדַּשְׁתּוֹ מִכָּל הַזְּמַנִּים,**

v'chayn kösuv b'sörösechö. **וְכֵן כָּתוּב בְּתוֹרָתֶךָ:**

You have consecrated to Your Name the Seventh Day, the purpose of the creation of heaven and earth. You have blessed it above all days and sanctified it above all festivals. And thus it is written in Your Torah:

Va-y'chulu ha-shöma-yim **וַיְכֻלּוּ הַשָּׁמַיִם**

v'hö-öretz v'chöl tz'vö-öm. **וְהָאָרֶץ וְכָל צְבָאָם:**

Va-y'chal elohim ba-yom **וַיְכַל אֱלֹהִים בַּיּוֹם**

ha-sh'vi-i, m'lachto asher **הַשְּׁבִיעִי, מְלַאכְתּוֹ אֲשֶׁר**

44

ösöh, va-yishbos ba-yom	עָשָׂה, וַיִּשְׁבֹּת בַּיּוֹם
ha-sh'vi-i miköl m'lachto	הַשְּׁבִיעִי מִכָּל מְלַאכְתּוֹ
asher ösöh. Va-y'vörech elohim	אֲשֶׁר עָשָׂה: וַיְבָרֶךְ אֱלֹהִים
es yom ha-sh'vi-i, va-y'kadaysh	אֶת יוֹם הַשְּׁבִיעִי וַיְקַדֵּשׁ
oso, ki vo shövas miköl	אֹתוֹ, כִּי בוֹ שָׁבַת מִכָּל
m'lachto, asher börö	מְלַאכְתּוֹ אֲשֶׁר בָּרָא
elohim la-asos.	אֱלֹהִים לַעֲשׂוֹת:

The heavens and the earth and all their hosts were completed. And God finished by the Seventh Day His work which He had done, and He rested on the Seventh Day from all His work which He had done. And God blessed the Seventh Day and made it holy, for on it He rested from all His work which God created to function.

Yis-m'chu v'mal'chus'chö	יִשְׂמְחוּ בְמַלְכוּתְךָ
shom'ray shabös v'kor'ay oneg,	שׁוֹמְרֵי שַׁבָּת וְקוֹרְאֵי עֹנֶג,
am m'kad'shay sh'vi-i, kulöm	עַם מְקַדְּשֵׁי שְׁבִיעִי, כֻּלָּם
yis-b'u v'yis-an'gu mituvechö,	יִשְׂבְּעוּ וְיִתְעַנְּגוּ מִטּוּבֶךָ,
uvash'vi-i rö-tzisö bo	וּבַשְּׁבִיעִי רָצִיתָ בּוֹ
v'kidashto, chemdas yömim	וְקִדַּשְׁתּוֹ, חֶמְדַּת יָמִים
oso köräsö, zaycher	אוֹתוֹ קָרָאתָ, זֵכֶר
l'ma-asay v'rayshis.	לְמַעֲשֵׂה בְרֵאשִׁית:

45

Those who observe the Shabbat and call it a delight shall rejoice in Your kingship; the nation which hallows the Seventh Day — all shall be satiated and delighted with Your goodness. You were pleased with the Seventh Day and made it holy; You called it the most desirable of days, in remembrance of the work of Creation.

Elohaynu vay-lohay avosay-nu,	אֱלֹהֵינוּ וֵאלֹהֵי אֲבוֹתֵינוּ,
r'tzay nö vim'nuchösaynu,	רְצֵה נָא בִמְנוּחָתֵנוּ,
kad'shaynu b'mitzvosechö	קַדְּשֵׁנוּ בְּמִצְוֹתֶיךָ
v'sayn chel-kaynu b'sorösechö,	וְתֵן חֶלְקֵנוּ בְּתוֹרָתֶךָ,
sab'aynu mi-tuvechö	שַׂבְּעֵנוּ מִטּוּבֶךָ
v'samay-ach naf-shaynu	וְשַׂמֵּחַ נַפְשֵׁנוּ
bishu-ösechö, v'tahayr libaynu	בִּישׁוּעָתֶךָ, וְטַהֵר לִבֵּנוּ
l'öv-d'chö be-emes,	לְעָבְדְּךָ בֶּאֱמֶת,
v'han-chi-laynu adonöy	וְהַנְחִילֵנוּ יְיָ
elohaynu b'ahavöh	אֱלֹהֵינוּ בְּאַהֲבָה
uv'rö-tzon shabas köd-shechö,	וּבְרָצוֹן שַׁבַּת קָדְשֶׁךָ,
v'yönuchu vöh köl yisrö-ayl	וְיָנוּחוּ בָהּ כָּל יִשְׂרָאֵל
m'kad'shay sh'mechö.	מְקַדְּשֵׁי שְׁמֶךָ׃
Boruch atöh adonöy,	בָּרוּךְ אַתָּה יְיָ,
m'kadaysh ha-shabös.	מְקַדֵּשׁ הַשַּׁבָּת׃

Our God and God of our fathers, please find favor in our rest, make us holy with Your commandments and grant us our portion in Your Torah; satiate us with Your goodness, gladden our soul with Your salvation, and make our heart pure to serve You in truth; and, Lord our God, grant as our heritage, in love and goodwill, Your holy Shabbat, and may all Israel who sanctify Your Name rest thereon. Blessed are You Lord, who sanctifies the Shabbat.

R'tzay, adonöy elohaynu,	רְצֵה, יְיָ אֱלֹהֵינוּ,
b'am'chö yisrö-ayl, v'lis'filösöm	בְּעַמְּךָ יִשְׂרָאֵל, וְלִתְפִלָּתָם
sh'ay, v'höshayv hö-avodöh	שְׁעֵה, וְהָשֵׁב הָעֲבוֹדָה
lid'vir bay-sechö, v'ishay	לִדְבִיר בֵּיתֶךָ, וְאִשֵּׁי
yisrö-ayl us'filösöm b'ahavöh	יִשְׂרָאֵל וּתְפִלָּתָם בְּאַהֲבָה
s'kabayl b'rö-tzon, us'hi	תְקַבֵּל בְּרָצוֹן, וּתְהִי
l'rö-tzon tömid avodas	לְרָצוֹן תָּמִיד עֲבוֹדַת
yisrö-ayl amechö.	יִשְׂרָאֵל עַמֶּךָ:

Look with favor, Lord our God, on Your people Israel and pay heed to their prayer; restore the service to Your Sanctuary and accept with love and favor Israel's fire-offerings and prayer; and may the service of Your people Israel always find favor.

On Rosh Chodesh and Festivals add:

Elohaynu vay-lohay avosaynu	אֱלֹהֵינוּ וֵאלֹהֵי אֲבוֹתֵינוּ
ya-aleh v'yövo, v'yagi-a v'yayrö-eh	יַעֲלֶה וְיָבֹא, וְיַגִּיעַ וְיֵרָאֶה
v'yay-rötzeh, v'yishöma v'yipökayd	וְיֵרָצֶה, וְיִשָּׁמַע וְיִפָּקֵד
v'yizöchayr, zichro-naynu	וְיִזָּכֵר, זִכְרוֹנֵנוּ

ufik'do-naynu, v'zichron	וּפָקְדוֹנֵנוּ, וְזִכְרוֹן
avosaynu, v'zichron möshi-ach	אֲבוֹתֵינוּ, וְזִכְרוֹן מָשִׁיחַ
ben dövid avdechö, v'zichron	בֶּן דָּוִד עַבְדֶּךָ, וְזִכְרוֹן
y'rushöla-yim ir köd-shechö,	יְרוּשָׁלַיִם עִיר קָדְשֶׁךָ,
v'zichron köl am'chö bays yisrö-ayl	וְזִכְרוֹן כָּל עַמְּךָ בֵּית יִשְׂרָאֵל
l'fönechö lif'laytöh l'tovöh, l'chayn	לְפָנֶיךָ לִפְלֵיטָה לְטוֹבָה, לְחֵן
ul'chesed ul'rachamim ul'cha-yim	וּלְחֶסֶד וּלְרַחֲמִים וּלְחַיִּים
tovim ul'shölom b'yom	טוֹבִים וּלְשָׁלוֹם, בְּיוֹם

On Rosh Chodesh:	בר״ח:
Rosh ha-chodesh ha-zeh.	רֹאשׁ הַחֹדֶשׁ הַזֶּה.
On Pesach:	בפסח:
Chag ha-matzos ha-zeh.	חַג הַמַּצּוֹת הַזֶּה.
On Sukkot:	בסוכות:
Chag ha-sukos ha-zeh.	חַג הַסֻּכּוֹת הַזֶּה.

Zöch'raynu adonöy elohaynu bo	זָכְרֵנוּ יְיָ אֱלֹהֵינוּ בּוֹ
l'tovöh, ufök'daynu vo liv'röchöh,	לְטוֹבָה, וּפָקְדֵנוּ בוֹ לִבְרָכָה,
v'hoshi-aynu vo l'cha-yim tovim.	וְהוֹשִׁיעֵנוּ בוֹ לְחַיִּים טוֹבִים;
Uvid'var y'shu-öh v'rachamim	וּבִדְבַר יְשׁוּעָה וְרַחֲמִים
chus v'chönaynu v'rachaym ölaynu	חוּס וְחָנֵּנוּ וְרַחֵם עָלֵינוּ
v'hoshi-aynu ki aylechö aynaynu,	וְהוֹשִׁיעֵנוּ כִּי אֵלֶיךָ עֵינֵינוּ,
ki ayl melech chanun	כִּי אֵל מֶלֶךְ חַנּוּן
v'rachum ötöh.	וְרַחוּם אָתָּה:

Our God and God of our fathers, may there ascend, come and reach, be seen, accepted, and heard, recalled and remembered before You, the remembrance and recollection of us, the remembrance of our fathers, the remembrance of *Moshiach* the son of David Your servant, the remembrance of Jerusalem Your holy city, and the remembrance of all Your people the House of Israel, for deliverance, well-being, grace, kindness, mercy, good life

48

and peace, on this day of: *On Rosh Chodesh:* Rosh Chodesh. *On Pesach:* the Festival of Matzot. *On Sukkot:* the Festival of Sukkot. Remember us on this [day], Lord our God, for good; be mindful of us on this [day] for blessing; help us on this [day] for good life. With the promise of deliverance and compassion, spare us and be gracious to us; have mercy upon us and deliver us; for our eyes are directed to You, for You, God, are a gracious and merciful King.

V'se-chezenöh aynaynu	וְתֶחֱזֶינָה עֵינֵינוּ
b'shuv'chö l'tziyon	בְּשׁוּבְךָ לְצִיּוֹן
b'rachamim. Böruch atöh	בְּרַחֲמִים. בָּרוּךְ אַתָּה
adonöy, ha-machazir	יְיָ, הַמַּחֲזִיר
sh'chinöso l'tziyon.	שְׁכִינָתוֹ לְצִיּוֹן׃

May our eyes behold Your return to Zion in mercy. Blessed are You Lord, who restores His Divine Presence to Zion.

Continue below. Level ⓑ resumes here.
Bow forward when saying the first five words of *Modim*.

Modim anachnu löch,	מוֹדִים אֲנַחְנוּ לָךְ,
shö-atöh hu adonöy elohaynu	שָׁאַתָּה הוּא יְיָ אֱלֹהֵינוּ
vay-lohay avosaynu l'olöm	וֵאלֹהֵי אֲבוֹתֵינוּ לְעוֹלָם
vö-ed, tzur cha-yaynu mögayn	וָעֶד, צוּר חַיֵּינוּ מָגֵן
yish-aynu, atöh hu l'dor	יִשְׁעֵנוּ, אַתָּה הוּא לְדוֹר

49

vödor, no-deh l'chö un'sapayr	וָדוֹר, נוֹדֶה לְךָ וּנְסַפֵּר
t'hilösechö, al cha-yaynu	תְּהִלָּתֶךָ, עַל חַיֵּינוּ
ha-m'surim b'yödechö,	הַמְּסוּרִים בְּיָדֶךָ,
v'al nish'mosaynu ha-p'kudos	וְעַל נִשְׁמוֹתֵינוּ הַפְּקוּדוֹת
löch, v'al nisechö sheb'chöl	לָךְ, וְעַל נִסֶּיךָ שֶׁבְּכָל
yom imönu, v'al nif-l'ösechö	יוֹם עִמָּנוּ, וְעַל נִפְלְאוֹתֶיךָ
v'tovosechö sheb'chöl ays erev	וְטוֹבוֹתֶיךָ שֶׁבְּכָל עֵת, עֶרֶב
vövoker v'tzöhörö-yim, ha-tov,	וָבֹקֶר וְצָהֳרָיִם, הַטּוֹב,
ki lo chölu ra-chamechö,	כִּי לֹא כָלוּ רַחֲמֶיךָ,
v'ham'rachaym, ki lo samu	וְהַמְרַחֵם, כִּי לֹא תַמּוּ
chasö-dechö, ki may-olöm	חֲסָדֶיךָ, כִּי מֵעוֹלָם
kivinu löch.	קִוִּינוּ לָךְ:

We thankfully acknowledge that You are the Lord our God and God of our fathers forever. You are the strength of our life, the shield of our salvation in every generation. We will give thanks to You and recount Your praise, evening, morning and noon, for our lives which are committed into Your hand, for our souls which are entrusted to You, for Your miracles which are with us daily, and for Your continual wonders and beneficences. You are the Beneficent One, for Your mercies never cease; and the Merciful One, for Your kindnesses never end; for we always place our hope in You.

During Chanukah add "V'al Hanisim" (see regular Siddur).
Otherwise continue below.

V'al kulöm yis-böraych   וְעַל כֻּלָּם יִתְבָּרֵךְ

v'yisromöm v'yisnasay   וְיִתְרוֹמָם וְיִתְנַשֵּׂא

shim'chö malkaynu   שִׁמְךָ מַלְכֵּנוּ

tömid l'olöm vö-ed.   תָּמִיד לְעוֹלָם וָעֶד:

And for all these, may Your Name, our King, be continually blessed, exalted and extolled forever and all time.

Between Rosh Hashana and Yom Kippur add:

Uch'sov l'cha-yim tovim   וּכְתוֹב לְחַיִּים טוֹבִים

köl b'nay v'risechö.   כָּל בְּנֵי בְרִיתֶךָ:

Inscribe all the children of Your Covenant for a good life.

At the words *Böruch* (blessed), bend the knee; at *Atöh* (You), bow forward; and at *Adonöy* (Lord), straighten up.

V'chöl ha-cha-yim yo-duchö   וְכֹל הַחַיִּים יוֹדוּךָ

selöh vihal'lu shim'chö   סֶּלָה וִיהַלְלוּ שִׁמְךָ

ha-gödol l'olöm ki tov,   הַגָּדוֹל לְעוֹלָם כִּי טוֹב,

hö-ayl y'shu-ösaynu   הָאֵל יְשׁוּעָתֵנוּ

v'ezrösaynu selöh, hö-ayl   וְעֶזְרָתֵנוּ סֶלָה, הָאֵל

ha-tov. Boruch atöh adonöy,   הַטּוֹב. בָּרוּךְ אַתָּה יְיָ,

51

ha-tov shim'chö ul'chö   הַטּוֹב שִׁמְךָ וּלְךָ
nö-eh l'hodos.   נָאֶה לְהוֹדוֹת:

And all living things shall forever thank You, and praise Your great Name eternally, for You are good. God, You are our everlasting salvation and help, O benevolent God. Blessed are You Lord, Beneficent is Your Name, and to You it is fitting to offer thanks.

Sim shölom tovöh uv'röchöh,	שִׂים שָׁלוֹם, טוֹבָה וּבְרָכָה,
cha-yim chayn vöchesed	חַיִּים חֵן וָחֶסֶד
v'rachamim, ölaynu v'al köl	וְרַחֲמִים, עָלֵינוּ וְעַל כָּל
yisrö-ayl amechö. Bö-r'chaynu	יִשְׂרָאֵל עַמֶּךָ. בָּרְכֵנוּ
övinu kulönu k'echöd,	אָבִינוּ כֻּלָּנוּ כְּאֶחָד,
b'or pönechö, ki v'or	בְּאוֹר פָּנֶיךָ, כִּי בְאוֹר
pönechö, nösatö lönu, adonöy	פָּנֶיךָ, נָתַתָּ לָנוּ יְיָ
elohaynu, toras cha-yim	אֱלֹהֵינוּ תּוֹרַת חַיִּים,
v'ahavas chesed utz'dököh	וְאַהֲבַת חֶסֶד, וּצְדָקָה
uv'röchöh v'rachamim	וּבְרָכָה וְרַחֲמִים
v'cha-yim v'shölom.	וְחַיִּים וְשָׁלוֹם.
V'tov b'aynechö l'vöraych es	וְטוֹב בְּעֵינֶיךָ לְבָרֵךְ אֶת

am'chö yisrö-ayl b'chöl ays עַמְּךָ יִשְׂרָאֵל בְּכָל עֵת

uv'chöl shö-öh bish'lomechö. וּבְכָל שָׁעָה בִּשְׁלוֹמֶךָ.

Bestow peace, goodness and blessing, life, graciousness, kindness and mercy, upon us and upon all Your people Israel. Bless us, our Father, all of us as one, with the light of Your countenance. For by the light of Your countenance You gave us, Lord our God, the Torah of life and loving-kindness, righteousness, blessing, mercy, life and peace. May it be favorable in Your eyes to bless Your people Israel, at all times and at every moment, with Your peace.

Between Rosh Hashana and Yom Kippur add:

Uv'sayfer cha-yim b'röchöh וּבְסֵפֶר חַיִּים בְּרָכָה

v'shölom ufarnösöh tovöh, וְשָׁלוֹם וּפַרְנָסָה טוֹבָה

y'shu-öh v'nechömöh, ug'zayros יְשׁוּעָה וְנֶחָמָה וּגְזֵרוֹת

tovos, nizöchayr v'nikösayv טוֹבוֹת נִזָּכֵר וְנִכָּתֵב

l'fönechö, anachnu v'chöl am'chö לְפָנֶיךָ, אֲנַחְנוּ וְכָל עַמְּךָ

bays yisrö-ayl, l'cha-yim בֵּית יִשְׂרָאֵל, לְחַיִּים

tovim ul'shölom. טוֹבִים וּלְשָׁלוֹם.

And in the Book of Life, blessing, peace and prosperity, deliverance, consolation and favorable decrees, may we and all Your people the House of Israel be remembered and inscribed before You for a happy life and for peace.

Boruch atöh adonöy, בָּרוּךְ אַתָּה יְיָ,

ha-m'vöraych es amo הַמְבָרֵךְ אֶת עַמּוֹ

yisrö-ayl ba-shölom. יִשְׂרָאֵל בַּשָּׁלוֹם׃

Blessed are You Lord, who blesses His people Israel with peace.

Yih-yu l'rö-tzon im'ray fi,   יִהְיוּ לְרָצוֹן אִמְרֵי פִי,

v'heg-yon libi l'fö-nechö,   וְהֶגְיוֹן לִבִּי לְפָנֶיךָ,

adonöy tzuri v'go-ali.   יְיָ צוּרִי וְגוֹאֲלִי.

May the words of my mouth and the meditation of my heart be acceptable before You, Lord, my Strength and my Redeemer.

Elohai, n'tzor l'shoni may-rö,   אֱלֹהַי, נְצוֹר לְשׁוֹנִי מֵרָע,

us'fösai midabayr mirmöh.   וּשְׂפָתַי מִדַּבֵּר מִרְמָה.

V'lim'kal'lai, nafshi sidom,   וְלִמְקַלְלַי, נַפְשִׁי תִדּוֹם,

v'nafshi ke-öför la-kol tih-yeh.   וְנַפְשִׁי כֶּעָפָר לַכֹּל תִּהְיֶה.

P'sach libi b'sorösechö,   פְּתַח לִבִּי בְּתוֹרָתֶךָ,

uv'mitzvosechö tirdof nafshi,   וּבְמִצְוֹתֶיךָ תִּרְדּוֹף נַפְשִׁי,

v'chöl ha-chosh'vim ölai rö-öh,   וְכָל הַחוֹשְׁבִים עָלַי רָעָה,

m'hayröh höfayr atzösöm   מְהֵרָה הָפֵר עֲצָתָם

v'kalkayl ma-chashavtöm.   וְקַלְקֵל מַחֲשַׁבְתָּם.

Yih-yu k'motz lif'nay ru-ach   יִהְיוּ כְּמוֹץ לִפְנֵי רוּחַ

umal-ach adonöy do-cheh.   וּמַלְאַךְ יְיָ דּוֹחֶה.

L'ma-an yay-chöl'tzun   לְמַעַן יֵחָלְצוּן

y'didechö, hoshi-öh y'min'chö   יְדִידֶיךָ, הוֹשִׁיעָה יְמִינְךָ

va-anayni. Asay l'ma-an   וַעֲנֵנִי. עֲשֵׂה לְמַעַן

sh'mechö, asay l'ma-an   שְׁמֶךָ, עֲשֵׂה לְמַעַן

y'minechö, asay l'ma-an   יְמִינֶךָ, עֲשֵׂה לְמַעַן

torösechö, asay l'ma-an   תּוֹרָתֶךָ, עֲשֵׂה לְמַעַן

k'dusho-sechö. Yih-yu   קְדֻשָּׁתֶךָ. יִהְיוּ

l'rö-tzon im'ray fi, v'heg-yon   לְרָצוֹן אִמְרֵי פִי, וְהֶגְיוֹן

libi l'fönechö, adonöy   לִבִּי לְפָנֶיךָ, יְיָ

tzuri v'go-ali.   צוּרִי וְגוֹאֲלִי.

My God, guard my tongue from evil and my lips from speaking deceitfully. Let my soul be silent to those who curse me; let my soul be as dust to all. Open my heart to Your Torah, and let my soul eagerly pursue Your commandments. As for all those who plot evil against me, hasten to annul their counsel and frustrate their design. Let them be as chaff before the wind; let the angel of the Lord thrust them away. That Your beloved ones may be delivered, help with Your right hand and answer me. Do it for the sake of Your Name; do it for the sake of Your right hand; do it for the sake of Your Torah; do it for the sake of Your holiness. May the words of my mouth and the meditation of my heart be acceptable before You, Lord, my Strength and my Redeemer.

Take three steps back and say:

O-seh shölom (*Between Rosh Hashana* (כש"ת: הַשָּׁלוֹם) עֹשֶׂה שָׁלוֹם

and Yom Kippur: ha-shölom) bim'romöv, בִּמְרוֹמָיו, הוּא יַעֲשֶׂה שָׁלוֹם

hu ya-aseh shölom ölaynu v'al עָלֵינוּ וְעַל כָּל יִשְׂרָאֵל,
köl yisrö-ayl, v'im'ru ömayn. וְאִמְרוּ אָמֵן:

He who makes peace (*Between Rosh Hashana and Yom Kippur substitute:* the peace) in His heavens, may He make peace for us and for all Israel; and say: Amen.

Y'hi rö-tzon mil'fönechö, adonöy יְהִי רָצוֹן מִלְּפָנֶיךָ, יְיָ
elohaynu vay-lohay avosaynu, אֱלֹהֵינוּ וֵאלֹהֵי אֲבוֹתֵינוּ,
she-yibö-neh bays ha-mikdösh שֶׁיִּבָּנֶה בֵּית הַמִּקְדָּשׁ
bim'hayröh v'yömaynu, בִּמְהֵרָה בְיָמֵינוּ,
v'sayn chelkaynu b'sorösechö. וְתֵן חֶלְקֵנוּ בְּתוֹרָתֶךָ.

May it be Your will, Lord our God and God of our fathers, that the *Beit Hamikdash* (Holy Temple) be speedily rebuilt in our days, and grant us our portion in Your Torah.

Take three steps forward.

Va-y'chulu... **For Levels:** 𝓑 𝓒   וַיְכֻלּוּ ...

Recited standing

Va-y'chulu ha-shöma-yim וַיְכֻלּוּ הַשָּׁמַיִם
v'hö-öretz v'chöl tz'vö-öm. וְהָאָרֶץ וְכָל צְבָאָם:
Va-y'chal elohim ba-yom וַיְכַל אֱלֹהִים בַּיּוֹם

ha-sh'vi-i, m'lachto asher	הַשְּׁבִיעִי, מְלַאכְתּוֹ אֲשֶׁר
ösöh, va-yishbos ba-yom	עָשָׂה, וַיִּשְׁבֹּת בַּיּוֹם
ha-sh'vi-i miköl m'lachto	הַשְּׁבִיעִי מִכָּל מְלַאכְתּוֹ
asher ösöh. Va-y'vörech elohim	אֲשֶׁר עָשָׂה: וַיְבָרֶךְ אֱלֹהִים
es yom ha-sh'vi-i, va-y'kadaysh	אֶת יוֹם הַשְּׁבִיעִי וַיְקַדֵּשׁ
oso, ki vo shövas miköl	אֹתוֹ, כִּי בוֹ שָׁבַת מִכָּל
m'lachto, asher börö	מְלַאכְתּוֹ אֲשֶׁר בָּרָא
elohim la-asos.	אֱלֹהִים לַעֲשׂוֹת:

These verses are from the first chapter in the Torah. By reciting them a Jew gives testimony that God created the heavens and the earth and all that is in them in six days, and rested on the seventh, which He proclaimed a holy day of rest.

Mögayn Övos..

For Levels: B C

מָגֵן אָבוֹת ...

Mögayn övos bid'vöro	מָגֵן אָבוֹת בִּדְבָרוֹ מְחַיֶּה
m'cha-yeh maysim b'ma-amöro,	מֵתִים בְּמַאֲמָרוֹ,
hö-ayl (bet. Rosh Hashana and Yom Kippur	הָאֵל (בש״ת הַמֶּלֶךְ)

substitute: ha-melech) ha-ködosh   הַקָּדוֹשׁ שֶׁאֵין

she-ayn kömohu, ha-mayni-ach   כָּמוֹהוּ, הַמֵּנִיחַ

l'amo b'yom shabbas   לְעַמּוֹ בְּיוֹם שַׁבַּת

köd-sho, ki vöm rötzöh   קָדְשׁוֹ, כִּי בָם רָצָה

l'höni-ach löhem, l'fönöv   לְהָנִיחַ לָהֶם, לְפָנָיו

na-avod b'yir-öh vö-fachad   נַעֲבוֹד בְּיִרְאָה וָפַחַד

v'no-deh lish'mo b'chöl yom   וְנוֹדֶה לִשְׁמוֹ בְּכָל יוֹם

tömid, may-ayn ha-b'röchos,   תָּמִיד, מֵעֵין הַבְּרָכוֹת,

ayl ha-hodö-os adon   אֵל הַהוֹדָאוֹת אֲדוֹן

ha-shölom, m'kadaysh   הַשָּׁלוֹם, מְקַדֵּשׁ

ha-shabös um'vöraych   הַשַּׁבָּת וּמְבָרֵךְ

sh'vi-i, umayni-ach bik'dushöh,   שְׁבִיעִי, וּמֵנִיחַ בִּקְדֻשָּׁה,

l'am m'dush'nay oneg, zaycher   לְעַם מְדֻשְּׁנֵי עֹנֶג, זֵכֶר

l'ma-asay v'rayshis.   לְמַעֲשֵׂה בְרֵאשִׁית:

This prayer speaks of the protection that God provides to His people. It also describes the greatness of God and how He gave us, the Jewish people, the Shabbat.

Between Pesach and Shavuot the *Omer* is counted here. Otherwise continue below.

Ölaynu...

For Levels:

Ⓑ Ⓒ

עָלֵינוּ ...

Ölaynu l'shabay-ach la-adon
ha-kol, lösays g'dulöh l'yo-tzayr
b'rayshis, shelo ösönu k'go-yay
hö-arö-tzos, v'lo sömönu
k'mish-p'chos hö-adömöh,
shelo söm chelkaynu köhem,
v'gorölaynu k'chöl ha-monöm
she-haym mishtachavim l'hevel
v'lörik. Va-anachnu kor'im
umish-tachavim umodim,
lif'nay melech, mal'chay
ha-m'löchim, ha-ködosh
böruch hu. She-hu noteh
shöma-yim v'yosayd ö-retz,
umoshav y'köro ba-shöma-yim

עָלֵינוּ לְשַׁבֵּחַ לַאֲדוֹן
הַכֹּל, לָתֵת גְּדֻלָּה לְיוֹצֵר
בְּרֵאשִׁית, שֶׁלֹּא עָשָׂנוּ כְּגוֹיֵי
הָאֲרָצוֹת, וְלֹא שָׂמָנוּ
כְּמִשְׁפְּחוֹת הָאֲדָמָה,
שֶׁלֹּא שָׂם חֶלְקֵנוּ כָּהֶם,
וְגֹרָלֵנוּ כְּכָל הֲמוֹנָם
שֶׁהֵם מִשְׁתַּחֲוִים לְהֶבֶל
וְלָרִיק. וַאֲנַחְנוּ כּוֹרְעִים
וּמִשְׁתַּחֲוִים וּמוֹדִים,
לִפְנֵי מֶלֶךְ, מַלְכֵי
הַמְּלָכִים, הַקָּדוֹשׁ
בָּרוּךְ הוּא. שֶׁהוּא נוֹטֶה
שָׁמַיִם וְיוֹסֵד אָרֶץ,
וּמוֹשַׁב יְקָרוֹ בַּשָּׁמַיִם

mima-al, ush'chinas uzo	מִמַּעַל, וּשְׁכִינַת עֻזּוֹ
b'göv'hay m'romim, hu	בְּגָבְהֵי מְרוֹמִים, הוּא
elohaynu ayn od. Emes	אֱלֹהֵינוּ אֵין עוֹד. אֱמֶת
malkaynu, efes zulöso,	מַלְכֵּנוּ, אֶפֶס זוּלָתוֹ,
kakösuv b'soröso: V'yöda-tö	כַּכָּתוּב בְּתוֹרָתוֹ : וְיָדַעְתָּ
ha-yom va-hashay-vosö el	הַיּוֹם וַהֲשֵׁבֹתָ אֶל
l'vövechö, ki adonöy hu	לְבָבֶךָ, כִּי יְיָ הוּא
hö-elohim ba-shöma-yim	הָאֱלֹהִים בַּשָּׁמַיִם
mima-al, v'al hö-öretz	מִמַּעַל, וְעַל הָאָרֶץ
mi-töchas, ayn od.	מִתָּחַת, אֵין עוֹד :

This is a very, very old prayer. The famous Rav Hai Gaon, the last of the Babylonian Geonim, states that this prayer was composed by Joshua, as he led the children of Israel into the Promised Land. (The initials of the first sentences, read backwards, form his original name "Hoshea.") Thus, when Joshua was about to settle the Jewish people in the Holy Land, he made them remember, through this prayer, that they were different from the other nations and tribes of the earth. It is a very important prayer, and everyone should be familiar with it. Jewish Law requires that when it is recited in the synagogue, everyone join in it, even if one has already said it, or just happened to walk into the synagogue at that time.

V'al kayn n'ka-veh l'chö	וְעַל כֵּן נְקַוֶּה לְךָ
adonöy elohaynu, lir-os	יְיָ אֱלֹהֵינוּ, לִרְאוֹת

m'hayröh b'sif-eres uzechö,	מְהֵרָה בְּתִפְאֶרֶת עֻזֶּךָ,
l'ha-avir gilulim min hö-öretz	לְהַעֲבִיר גִּלּוּלִים מִן הָאָרֶץ
v'hö-elilim köros yiköray-sun,	וְהָאֱלִילִים כָּרוֹת יִכָּרֵתוּן,
l'sakayn olöm b'mal'chus	לְתַקֵּן עוֹלָם בְּמַלְכוּת
shadai, v'chöl b'nay vösör	שַׁדַּי, וְכָל בְּנֵי בָשָׂר
yik-r'u vish'mechö, l'hafnos	יִקְרְאוּ בִשְׁמֶךָ, לְהַפְנוֹת
ay-lechö köl rish'ay öretz.	אֵלֶיךָ כָּל רִשְׁעֵי אָרֶץ.
Yakiru v'yay-d'u köl yosh'vay	יַכִּירוּ וְיֵדְעוּ כָּל יוֹשְׁבֵי
sayvayl, ki l'chö tichra köl	תֵבֵל, כִּי לְךָ תִּכְרַע כָּל
berech, tishöva köl löshon.	בֶּרֶךְ, תִּשָּׁבַע כָּל לָשׁוֹן.
L'fönechö adonöy elohaynu	לְפָנֶיךָ יְיָ אֱלֹהֵינוּ
yich-r'u v'yipolu, v'lich'vod	יִכְרְעוּ וְיִפֹּלוּ, וְלִכְבוֹד
shim'chö y'kör yitaynu,	שִׁמְךָ יְקָר יִתֵּנוּ,
vi-kab'lu chulöm alay-hem es	וִיקַבְּלוּ כֻלָּם עֲלֵיהֶם אֶת
ol mal'chusechö, v'simloch	עוֹל מַלְכוּתֶךָ, וְתִמְלוֹךְ
alayhem m'hayröh l'olöm	עֲלֵיהֶם מְהֵרָה לְעוֹלָם
vö-ed, ki ha-mal'chus shel'chö	וָעֶד, כִּי הַמַּלְכוּת שֶׁלְּךָ
hi, ul'ol'may ad timloch	הִיא, וּלְעוֹלְמֵי עַד תִּמְלוֹךְ
b'chövod, ka-kösuv	בְּכָבוֹד, כַּכָּתוּב

b'chövod, ka-kösuv בִּכְבוֹד, כַּכָּתוּב

b'sorösechö, adonöy yimloch בְּתוֹרָתֶךָ: יְיָ יִמְלֹךְ

l'olöm vö-ed. V'ne-emar, לְעֹלָם וָעֶד. וְנֶאֱמַר:

v'hö-yöh adonöy l'melech al וְהָיָה יְיָ לְמֶלֶךְ עַל

köl hö-öretz, ba-yom כָּל הָאָרֶץ, בַּיוֹם

hahu yih-yeh adonöy הַהוּא יִהְיֶה יְיָ

echöd ush'mo echöd. אֶחָד וּשְׁמוֹ אֶחָד:

In this prayer we express our hope for that Great Day when all the people of the earth will recognize God.

Al tirö mipachad pis-om, אַל תִּירָא מִפַּחַד פִּתְאֹם,

umisho-as r'shö-im ki sövo. Utzu וּמִשֹּׁאַת רְשָׁעִים כִּי תָבֹא: עֻצוּ

ay-tzöh v'suför, dab'ru dövör v'lo עֵצָה וְתֻפָר, דַּבְּרוּ דָבָר וְלֹא

yökum, ki imönu ayl. V'ad יָקוּם, כִּי עִמָּנוּ אֵל: וְעַד

zik-nöh ani hu, v'ad sayvöh ani זִקְנָה אֲנִי הוּא, וְעַד שֵׂיבָה אֲנִי

esbol, ani ösisi va-ani אֶסְבֹּל, אֲנִי עָשִׂיתִי וַאֲנִי

esö, va-ani esbol va-amalayt. אֶשָּׂא, וַאֲנִי אֶסְבֹּל וַאֲמַלֵּט:

Ach tzadikim yodu lish'mechö אַךְ צַדִּיקִים יוֹדוּ לִשְׁמֶךָ

yay-sh'vu y'shörim es pönechö. יֵשְׁבוּ יְשָׁרִים אֶת פָּנֶיךָ:

These meaningful verses remind us that God will always protect us.

Going to Sleep/Waking Up

Before going to sleep we recite a special set of prayers referred to as "*Kriat Shema*." This includes the Shema (on page 32) and a few other prayers (which can be found in a regular "Siddur" prayer book.) It is also customary to prepare a cup of water and a small bowl or basin near the bed with which you'll wash your hands upon waking in the morning. Some also have the custom to kiss the Mezuzah on the door to the bedroom.

Upon waking, recite the *Modeh Ani* (see next page), and wash your hands with the cup of water you prepared the night before (this washing is separate from the washing found at the beginning of the Morning Blessings).

Directions for washing the hands: Take the cup in the right hand, pass it to the left hand, and pour over the right hand. Now, take the cup with the right hand and pour over the entire left hand. Repeat the process two more times (for a total of three pourings on each hand). Do not recite any blessing for this washing.

After this first washing of the hands you may alight from bed, get dressed and recite the Morning Blessings (on page 65), beginning with the Washing of the Hands.

The Morning Blessings

The first thing we become aware of when we awake from our sleep is that we are awake and alive, and so we thank God for this and express our appreciation by reciting the Morning Blessings.

The earliest moments of the day are like the first of our fruits, which we reserve and dedicate to God. Our Sages taught us that the way we begin our day, that's the way the day will go. So by beginning it with blessings and prayer we ensure that the entire day will be permeated with goodness and holiness.

The Morning Blessings are followed by the Morning Service, (see page 80).

Modeh Ani...	**For Levels:** 𝒜 ℬ 𝒞	מוֹדֶה אֲנִי ...

As soon as you wake up, recite the following:

Modeh ani l'fönechö   מוֹדֶה אֲנִי לְפָנֶיךָ

melech chai v'kayöm,   מֶלֶךְ חַי וְקַיָּם,

64

she-heche-zartö bi   שֶׁהֶחֱזַרְתָּ בִּי

nish'mösi b'chemlö,   נִשְׁמָתִי בְּחֶמְלָה,

raböh emunösechö.   רַבָּה אֱמוּנָתֶךְ:

I thank you, living and eternal King, for giving me back my soul. Your faithfulness is great.

N'tilas Yödö-yim... **For Levels:** *A B C*   נְטִילַת יָדַיִם...

Fill a large cup with water. Take the cup in the right hand, pass it to the left hand, and pour over the entire right hand (until the wrist). Now, take the cup with the right hand and pour over the entire left hand. Repeat the process two more times (for a total of three pourings on each hand). Rub your hands together and recite the blessing below, then dry your hands.

Böruch atöh adonöy,   בָּרוּךְ אַתָּה יְיָ,

elohaynu melech hö-olöm,   אֱלֹהֵינוּ מֶלֶךְ הָעוֹלָם,

asher kid'shönu b'mitzvosöv,   אֲשֶׁר קִדְּשָׁנוּ בְּמִצְוֹתָיו,

v'tzivönu al n'tilas yödö-yim.   וְצִוָּנוּ עַל נְטִילַת יָדַיִם:

Blessed are You, Lord our God, King of the universe, who has made us holy with His mitzvot, and commanded us to wash our hands.

65

Asher Yötzar ...   **For Levels:** Ⓑ Ⓒ   אֲשֶׁר יָצַר ...

Did you know? The follwing blessing is also recited anytime you leave the restroom (after washing the hands).

Böruch atöh adonöy	בָּרוּךְ אַתָּה יְיָ,
elohaynu melech hö-olöm,	אֱלֹהֵינוּ מֶלֶךְ הָעוֹלָם,
asher yötzar es hö-ö-döm	אֲשֶׁר יָצַר אֶת הָאָדָם
b'chöchmöh, uvörö vo	בְּחָכְמָה, וּבָרָא בוֹ
n'kövim n'kövim, cha-lulim	נְקָבִים נְקָבִים, חֲלוּלִים
cha-lulim, göluy v'yödu-a	חֲלוּלִים, גָּלוּי וְיָדוּעַ
lif'nay chisay ch'vodechö,	לִפְנֵי כִסֵּא כְבוֹדֶךָ,
she-im yisösaym echöd	שֶׁאִם יִסָּתֵם אֶחָד
may-hem, o im yi-pösay-ach	מֵהֶם, אוֹ אִם יִפָּתֵחַ
echöd may-hem, ee efshar	אֶחָד מֵהֶם, אִי אֶפְשַׁר
l'hiska-yaym afilu shö-öh	לְהִתְקַיֵּם אֲפִלּוּ שָׁעָה
echös. Böruch atöh adonöy,	אֶחָת. בָּרוּךְ אַתָּה יְיָ,
rofay chöl bösör	רוֹפֵא כָל בָּשָׂר
umafli la-asos.	וּמַפְלִיא לַעֲשׂוֹת:

66

Blessed are You, Lord our God, King of the universe, Who has created us with a body that works so well. You know that even if one part of our body is blocked and does not work properly, it would be impossible for us to live.

Elohai, N'shömöh...　　**For Levels:**　　... אֱלֹהַי, נְשָׁמָה

                      ᏻ

Hebrew	Transliteration
אֱלֹהַי, נְשָׁמָה שֶׁנָּתַתָּ	Elohai, n'shömöh she-nösatö
בִּי טְהוֹרָה הִיא, אַתָּה	bi t'horöh hi, atöh
בְרָאתָהּ, אַתָּה יְצַרְתָּהּ,	v'rösöh, atöh y'tzartöh,
אַתָּה נְפַחְתָּהּ בִּי, וְאַתָּה	atöh n'fachtöh bi, v'atöh
מְשַׁמְּרָהּ בְּקִרְבִּי, וְאַתָּה	m'sham'röh b'kirbi, v'atöh
עָתִיד לִטְּלָהּ מִמֶּנִּי,	ösid lit'löh mimeni,
וּלְהַחֲזִירָהּ בִּי לֶעָתִיד לָבֹא.	ul'hacha-ziröh bi le-ösid lövo.
כָּל זְמַן שֶׁהַנְּשָׁמָה	Köl z'man she-han'shömöh
בְּקִרְבִּי, מוֹדֶה אֲנִי לְפָנֶיךָ	b'kirbi, modeh ani l'fönechö
יְיָ אֱלֹהַי וֵאלֹהֵי אֲבוֹתַי,	adonöy elohai velohay avosai,
רִבּוֹן כָּל הַמַּעֲשִׂים, אֲדוֹן	ribon köl hama-asim, adon
כָּל הַנְּשָׁמוֹת. בָּרוּךְ אַתָּה	köl ha-n'shömos. Böruch atöh

adonöy, ha-machazir נְשָׁמוֹת הַמַּחֲזִיר יְיָ,

n'shömos lif'gorim maysim. מֵתִים: לִפְגָרִים

The soul that You have placed within me is pure. As long as I have the breath of life I offer thanks to You, Lord of all souls.

Birchos Ha-shachar **For Levels:** Ⓑ Ⓒ   בִּרְכוֹת הַשַּׁחַר

As Jews, we see God's hand in every one of the innumerable wonders of Nature. Every morning we take time to acknowledge the great miracles that God performs for us on a daily basis. Nature, too, is a miracle, for what seems natural is only because we are accustomed to it, however, it is truly a constantly renewing miracle from God.

Recited Standing

Böruch atöh adonöy, בָּרוּךְ אַתָּה יְיָ,

elohaynu melech hö-olöm, אֱלֹהֵינוּ מֶלֶךְ הָעוֹלָם,

hanosayn lasechvi vinöh הַנּוֹתֵן לַשֶּׂכְוִי בִינָה

l'havchin bayn yom לְהַבְחִין בֵּין יוֹם

uvayn löy-löh. וּבֵין לָיְלָה:

Blessed are You, Lord our God, King of the universe, who gives the rooster understanding to distinguish between day and night.

68

Böruch atöh adonöy, בָּרוּךְ אַתָּה יְיָ,

elohaynu melech hö-olöm, אֱלֹהֵינוּ מֶלֶךְ הָעוֹלָם,

pokay-ach iv'rim. פּוֹקֵחַ עִוְרִים:

Blessed are You, Lord our God, King of the universe, who opens the eyes of the blind.

Böruch atöh adonöy, בָּרוּךְ אַתָּה יְיָ,

elohaynu melech hö-olöm, אֱלֹהֵינוּ מֶלֶךְ הָעוֹלָם,

matir asurim. מַתִּיר אֲסוּרִים:

Blessed are You, Lord our God, King of the universe, who releases the bound.

Böruch atöh adonöy, בָּרוּךְ אַתָּה יְיָ,

elohaynu melech hö-olöm, אֱלֹהֵינוּ מֶלֶךְ הָעוֹלָם,

zo-kayf k'fufim. זוֹקֵף כְּפוּפִים:

Blessed are You, Lord our God, King of the universe, who straightens the bowed.

Böruch atöh adonöy, בָּרוּךְ אַתָּה יְיָ,

elohaynu melech hö-olöm, אֱלֹהֵינוּ מֶלֶךְ הָעוֹלָם,

malbish aru-mim. מַלְבִּישׁ עֲרֻמִּים:

Blessed are You, Lord our God, King of the universe, who clothes the naked.

69

Böruch atöh adonöy, בָּרוּךְ אַתָּה יְיָ,

elohaynu melech hö-olöm, אֱלֹהֵינוּ מֶלֶךְ הָעוֹלָם,

ha-nosayn la-yö-ayf ko-ach. הַנּוֹתֵן לַיָּעֵף כֹּחַ:

Blessed are You, Lord our God, King of the universe, who gives strength to the weary.

Böruch atöh adonöy, בָּרוּךְ אַתָּה יְיָ,

elohaynu melech hö-olöm, אֱלֹהֵינוּ מֶלֶךְ הָעוֹלָם,

roka hö-öretz al ha-möyim. רוֹקַע הָאָרֶץ עַל הַמָּיִם:

Blessed are You, Lord our God, King of the universe, who spreads forth the earth above the waters.

Böruch atöh adonöy, בָּרוּךְ אַתָּה יְיָ,

elohaynu melech hö-olöm, אֱלֹהֵינוּ מֶלֶךְ הָעוֹלָם,

ha-may-chin mitz-aday göver. הַמֵּכִין מִצְעֲדֵי גָבֶר:

Blessed are You, Lord our God, King of the universe, who directs the steps of man.

Böruch atöh adonöy, בָּרוּךְ אַתָּה יְיָ,

elohaynu melech hö-olöm, אֱלֹהֵינוּ מֶלֶךְ הָעוֹלָם,

she-ösöh lee köl tzörki. שֶׁעָשָׂה לִי כָּל צָרְכִּי:

Blessed are You, Lord our God, King of the universe, who has provided me with my every need.

Böruch atöh adonöy, בָּרוּךְ אַתָּה יְיָ,

elohaynu melech hö-olöm, אֱלֹהֵינוּ מֶלֶךְ הָעוֹלָם,

o-zayr yisrö-ayl big'vuröh. אוֹזֵר יִשְׂרָאֵל בִּגְבוּרָה:

Blessed are You, Lord our God, King of the universe, who girds [the people] Israel with might.

Böruch atöh adonöy, בָּרוּךְ אַתָּה יְיָ,

elohaynu melech hö-olöm, אֱלֹהֵינוּ מֶלֶךְ הָעוֹלָם,

o-tayr yisrö-ayl b'sif-öröh. עוֹטֵר יִשְׂרָאֵל בְּתִפְאָרָה:

Blessed are You, Lord our God, King of the universe, who crowns [the people] Israel with glory.

Böruch atöh adonöy, בָּרוּךְ אַתָּה יְיָ,

elohaynu melech hö-olöm, אֱלֹהֵינוּ מֶלֶךְ הָעוֹלָם,

shelo ösani goy. שֶׁלֹא עָשַׂנִי גּוֹי:

Blessed are You, Lord our God, King of the universe, who has not made me a gentile.

Böruch atöh adonöy, בָּרוּךְ אַתָּה יְיָ,

elohaynu melech hö-olöm, אֱלֹהֵינוּ מֶלֶךְ הָעוֹלָם,

shelo ösani öved. :שֶׁלֹּא עָשַׂנִי עָבֶד

Blessed are You, Lord our God, King of the universe, who has not made me a slave.

Men and boys recite the following blessing:

Böruch atöh adonöy, ,בָּרוּךְ אַתָּה יְיָ

elohaynu melech hö-olöm, ,אֱלֹהֵינוּ מֶלֶךְ הָעוֹלָם

shelo ösani ishöh. :שֶׁלֹּא עָשַׂנִי אִשָּׁה

Blessed are You, Lord our God, King of the universe, who has not made me a woman (who is exempt from certain mitzvos).

ha-ma-avir...   **For Levels:**   ...הַמַּעֲבִיר שֵׁנָה

ⓖ

Böruch atöh adonöy, ,בָּרוּךְ אַתָּה יְיָ

elohaynu melech hö-olöm, ,אֱלֹהֵינוּ מֶלֶךְ הָעוֹלָם

ha-ma-avir shay-nöh הַמַּעֲבִיר שֵׁנָה

may-aynöy us'numöh מֵעֵינַי וּתְנוּמָה

may-af-apöy. :מֵעַפְעַפָּי

Blessed are You, Lord our God, King of the universe, who removes sleep from my eyes and slumber from my eyelids.

Vi-hi rötzon mil'fönechö	וִיהִי רָצוֹן מִלְּפָנֶיךָ
adonöy elo-haynu vay-lohay	יְיָ אֱלֹהֵינוּ וֵאלֹהֵי
avo-saynu, she-targilaynu	אֲבוֹתֵינוּ, שֶׁתַּרְגִּילֵנוּ
b'sorösechö, v'sadbikaynu	בְּתוֹרָתֶךָ, וְתַדְבִּיקֵנוּ
b'mitzvosechö, v'al t'vi-aynu	בְּמִצְוֹתֶיךָ, וְאַל תְּבִיאֵנוּ
lo li-day chayt, vlo li-day	לֹא לִידֵי חֵטְא, וְלֹא לִידֵי
avay-röh v'övon, v'lo li-day	עֲבֵרָה וְעָוֹן, וְלֹא לִידֵי
nisö-yon v'lo li-day vizö-yon,	נִסָּיוֹן וְלֹא לִידֵי בִזָּיוֹן,
v'al yishlot bönu yaytzer hörö,	וְאַל יִשְׁלוֹט בָּנוּ יֵצֶר הָרָע,
v'har-chikaynu may-ödöm rö,	וְהַרְחִיקֵנוּ מֵאָדָם רָע,
umay-chövayr rö, v'dab'kaynu	וּמֵחָבֵר רָע, וְדַבְּקֵנוּ
b'yaytzer tov uv'ma-asim	בְּיֵצֶר טוֹב וּבְמַעֲשִׂים
tovim, v'chof es yitzraynu	טוֹבִים, וְכוֹף אֶת יִצְרֵנוּ
l'hish-ta-bed löch, us'naynu	לְהִשְׁתַּעְבֶּד לָךְ, וּתְנֵנוּ
ha-yom uv'chöl yom l'chayn	הַיּוֹם וּבְכָל יוֹם לְחֵן
ul'chesed ul'rachamim	וּלְחֶסֶד וּלְרַחֲמִים
b'ay-nechö uv'aynay chöl	בְּעֵינֶיךָ וּבְעֵינֵי כָל
ro-aynu, v'sig-m'laynu	רוֹאֵינוּ, וְתִגְמְלֵנוּ

חֲסָדִים טוֹבִים. בָּרוּךְ אַתָּה
יְיָ, הַגּוֹמֵל חֲסָדִים
טוֹבִים לְעַמּוֹ יִשְׂרָאֵל׃

chasödim tovim. Böruch atöh adonöy, ha-gomayl chasödim tovim l'amo yisrö-ayl.

And may it be Your will, Lord our God and God of our fathers, to accustom us to [study] Your Torah, and to make us cleave to Your commandments. Do not bring us into sin, nor into transgression or iniquity, nor into temptation or scorn; and may the evil inclination not have mastery over us.

יְהִי רָצוֹן מִלְּפָנֶיךָ
יְיָ אֱלֹהַי וֵאלֹהֵי
אֲבוֹתַי, שֶׁתַּצִּילֵנִי הַיּוֹם
וּבְכָל יוֹם מֵעַזֵּי פָנִים,
וּמֵעַזּוּת פָּנִים, מֵאָדָם
רָע, וּמֵחָבֵר רָע,
וּמִשָּׁכֵן רָע, וּמִפֶּגַע רָע,
מֵעַיִן הָרָע, מִלָּשׁוֹן הָרָע,
מִמַּלְשִׁינוּת, מֵעֵדוּת
שֶׁקֶר, מִשִּׂנְאַת הַבְּרִיּוֹת,
מֵעֲלִילָה, מִמִּיתָה

Vi-hi rötzon mil'fönechö adonöy elo-hai vay-lohay avosai, sheta-tzilayni ha-yom uv'chöl yom may-azay fönim, umay-azus pönim, may-ödöm rö, umay-chövayr rö, umishö-chayn rö, umipega rö, may-ayin hörö, mi-löshon hörö, mima-lshinus, may-aydus sheker, misin-as hab'riyos, may-alilöh, mimi-söh

74

m'shunöh, may-chölö-yim	מְשֻׁנָּה, מֵחֳלָיִם
rö-im, umimikrim rö-im,	רָעִים, וּמִמִּקְרִים רָעִים,
umisötön hamash-chis, midin	וּמִשָּׂטָן הַמַּשְׁחִית, מִדִּין
kösheh, umiba-al din kösheh,	קָשֶׁה, וּמִבַּעַל דִּין קָשֶׁה,
bayn shehu ven b'ris, uvayn	בֵּין שֶׁהוּא בֶן בְּרִית, וּבֵין
she-ayno ven b'ris, umidinöh	שֶׁאֵינוֹ בֶן בְּרִית, וּמִדִּינָהּ
shel gay-hinom.	שֶׁל גֵּיהִנֹּם:

May it be Your will, Lord my God and God of my fathers, to protect me this day and every day from a wicked man, from an evil companion, from an evil neighbor and from an evil occurrence; from unnatural death, from harsh diseases and from misfortune; from the destructive adversary, from a harsh judgment, and from the retribution of gehinom.

Birkas Hatoröh — בִּרְכַּת הַתּוֹרָה

For Levels:
Ⓐ Ⓑ Ⓒ

Böruch atöh adonöy,	בָּרוּךְ אַתָּה יְיָ,
elohaynu melech hö-olöm,	אֱלֹהֵינוּ מֶלֶךְ הָעוֹלָם,
asher kid'shönu b'mitzvosöv,	אֲשֶׁר קִדְּשָׁנוּ בְּמִצְוֹתָיו,
v'tzivönu al div'ray soröh.	וְצִוָּנוּ עַל דִּבְרֵי תוֹרָה:

Blessed are You, Lord our God, King of the universe, who has sanctified us

with His commandments, and commanded us concerning the words of the Torah.

V'ha-arev nö adonöy	וְהַעֲרֶב נָא יְיָ
elo-haynu es div'ray so-rös'chö	אֱלֹהֵינוּ אֶת דִּבְרֵי תוֹרָתְךָ
b'finu, uv'fi chöl am'chö bays	בְּפִינוּ, וּבְפִי כָל עַמְּךָ בֵּית
yisrö-ayl, v'nih-yeh anachnu	יִשְׂרָאֵל, וְנִהְיֶה אֲנַחְנוּ
v'tze-etzö-ynu, v'tze-etzö-ay	וְצֶאֱצָאֵינוּ, וְצֶאֱצָאֵי
chöl am'chö bays yisrö-ayl,	כָל עַמְּךָ בֵּית יִשְׂרָאֵל,
kulönu yod'ay sh'mechö	כֻּלָּנוּ יוֹדְעֵי שְׁמֶךָ
v'lom'day sorös'chö lish'möh.	וְלוֹמְדֵי תוֹרָתְךָ לִשְׁמָהּ.
Böruch atöh adonöy,	בָּרוּךְ אַתָּה יְיָ,
ha-m'lamayd toröh	הַמְלַמֵּד תּוֹרָה
l'amo yisrö-ayl.	לְעַמּוֹ יִשְׂרָאֵל:

May we and our children and the children of Your entire people, the House of Israel, all be knowers of Your Name and students of Your Torah.

Böruch atöh adonöy	בָּרוּךְ אַתָּה יְיָ,
elohaynu melech hö-olöm,	אֱלֹהֵינוּ מֶלֶךְ הָעוֹלָם,
asher böchar bönu mi-köl	אֲשֶׁר בָּחַר בָּנוּ מִכָּל

hö-amim, v'nösan lönu es הָעַמִּים וְנָתַן לָנוּ אֶת

toröso. Böruch atöh adonöy, תּוֹרָתוֹ. בָּרוּךְ אַתָּה יְיָ,

nosayn ha-toröh. נוֹתֵן הַתּוֹרָה:

Blessed are You, Lord our God, King of the universe, who has chosen us from among all the nations and given us His Torah.

Levels Ⓑ Ⓒ continue here:

Va-y'dabayr adonöy el moshe וַיְדַבֵּר יְיָ אֶל מֹשֶׁה

laymor. Da-bayr el aharon v'el לֵּאמֹר: דַּבֵּר אֶל אַהֲרֹן וְאֶל

bönöv laymor, ko s'vö-r'chu בָּנָיו לֵאמֹר, כֹּה תְבָרְכוּ

es b'nay yisrö-ayl, ömor אֶת בְּנֵי יִשְׂרָאֵל, אָמוֹר

löhem. Y'vörech'chö adonöy לָהֶם: יְבָרֶכְךָ יְיָ

v'yish-m'rechö. Yö-ayr adonöy וְיִשְׁמְרֶךָ: יָאֵר יְיָ

pönöv ay-lechö vi-chunekö. פָּנָיו אֵלֶיךָ וִיחֻנֶּךָ:

Yisö adonöy pönöv aylechö יִשָּׂא יְיָ פָּנָיו אֵלֶיךָ

v'yösaym l'chö shölom. וְיָשֵׂם לְךָ שָׁלוֹם:

V'sömu es sh'mi al b'nay וְשָׂמוּ אֶת שְׁמִי עַל בְּנֵי

yisrö-ayl, va'ani avö-r'chaym. יִשְׂרָאֵל, וַאֲנִי אֲבָרְכֵם:

And the Lord spoke to Moses, saying: Speak to Aaron and to his sons,

saying, thus shall you bless the children of Israel; say to them: The Lord bless you and guard you. The Lord make His countenance shine upon you and be gracious to you. The Lord turn His countenance toward you and grant you peace. And they shall set My name upon the children of Israel, and I shall bless them.

Level 𝒢 continue here:

Aylu d'vörim she-ayn	אֵלּוּ דְבָרִים שֶׁאֵין
löhem shi-ur: Ha-payöh,	לָהֶם שִׁעוּר: הַפֵּאָה,
v'ha-bikurim, v'hö-r'öyon,	וְהַבִּכּוּרִים, וְהָרְאָיוֹן,
ug'milus chasödim, v'salmud	וּגְמִילוּת חֲסָדִים, וְתַלְמוּד
toröh. Aylu d'vörim she-ödöm	תּוֹרָה: אֵלּוּ דְבָרִים שֶׁאָדָם
ochayl payro-sayhem bö-olöm	אוֹכֵל פֵּרוֹתֵיהֶם בָּעוֹלָם
ha-zeh v'ha-keren ka-yemes	הַזֶּה וְהַקֶּרֶן קַיֶּמֶת
lö-olöm habö, v'aylu hayn:	לָעוֹלָם הַבָּא, וְאֵלּוּ הֵן:
Kibud öv vö-aym, ug'milus	כִּבּוּד אָב וָאֵם, וּגְמִילוּת
chasödim, v'hashkömas bays	חֲסָדִים, וְהַשְׁכָּמַת בֵּית
ha-midrösh sha-charis v'ar'vis,	הַמִּדְרָשׁ שַׁחֲרִית וְעַרְבִית,
v'hachnösas or'chim, uvikur	וְהַכְנָסַת אוֹרְחִים, וּבִקּוּר
cholim, v'hachnösas kalöh,	חוֹלִים, וְהַכְנָסַת כַּלָּה,

v'halvö-yas ha-mays, v'iyun	וְהַלְוָיַת הַמֵּת, וְעִיּוּן
t'filöh, va-havö-as shölom	תְּפִלָּה, וַהֲבָאַת שָׁלוֹם
she-bayn ödöm la-chavayro,	שֶׁבֵּין אָדָם לַחֲבֵרוֹ,
uvayn ish l'ishto, v'salmud	וּבֵין אִישׁ לְאִשְׁתּוֹ, וְתַלְמוּד
toröh k'neged kulöm.	תּוֹרָה כְּנֶגֶד כֻּלָּם:

These are the precepts, the fruits of which man enjoys in this world, while the principal [reward] remains in the World to Come: Honoring one's father and mother, performing deeds of kindness, early attendance at the House of Study morning and evening, hospitality to strangers, visiting the sick, dowering the bride, escorting the dead, concentration in prayer, bringing peace between man and his fellowman and between husband and wife.

Bir'kas Tzitzis   **For Levels:**   בִּרְכַּת צִיצִית

Ⓐ Ⓑ Ⓒ

Boys customarily begin wearing Tzitzit from the age of three and onward. Before reciting the blessing, gather all four fringes in the right hand (left-handed people hold them in the left hand). After making the blessing, bring the fringes to the lips and kiss them, then release them.

Böruch atöh adonöy	בָּרוּךְ אַתָּה יְיָ,
elohaynu melech hö-olöm,	אֱלֹהֵינוּ מֶלֶךְ הָעוֹלָם,

79

asher kid'shönu b'mitzvosöv, אֲשֶׁר קִדְּשָׁנוּ בְּמִצְוֹתָיו,

v'tzivönu al mitzvas tzitzis. וְצִוָּנוּ עַל מִצְוַת צִיצִית:

Blessed are You, Lord our God, King of the universe, who has sanctified us with His commandments, and commanded us to enwrap ourselves with tzitzit.

The Shabbat Morning Service

Ha-Rayni M'kabel...   **For Levels:**   הֲרֵינִי מְקַבֵּל...
𝓐 𝓑 𝓒

Harayni m'kabayl ölai mitzvas הֲרֵינִי מְקַבֵּל עָלַי מִצְוַת

asai shel v'öhavtö עֲשֵׂה שֶׁל: וְאָהַבְתָּ

l'ray-achö kö-mochö. לְרֵעֲךָ כָּמוֹךָ:

I hereby take upon myself to fulfill the mitzvah, "Love your fellowman as yourself."

Mah Tovu...   **For Levels:**   מַה טֹבוּ ...
𝓐 𝓑 𝓒

Mah tovu ohölechö ya-akov, מַה טֹּבוּ אֹהָלֶיךָ יַעֲקֹב,

mish-k'nosechö yisrö-ayl. מִשְׁכְּנֹתֶיךָ יִשְׂרָאֵל:

Va-ani b'rov chas-d'chö övo	וַאֲנִי בְּרֹב חַסְדְּךָ אָבֹא
vaysechö, eshta-chaveh el	בֵיתֶךָ, אֶשְׁתַּחֲוֶה אֶל
haychal köd-sh'chö b'yir-ösecho.	הֵיכַל קָדְשְׁךָ בְּיִרְאָתֶךָ:
Va-ani s'filösi l'chö adonöy ays	וַאֲנִי תְפִלָּתִי לְךָ יְיָ עֵת
rötzon, elohim b'röv chasdechö,	רָצוֹן, אֱלֹהִים בְּרָב חַסְדֶּךָ,
anay-ni be-emes yish-echö.	עֲנֵנִי בֶּאֱמֶת יִשְׁעֶךָ:

How goodly are your tents, O Jacob, your dwelling places, O Israel! And I, through Your abundant kindness, come into your house; I bow toward Your holy sanctuary in awe of You. May my prayer to You, Lord, be at a propitious time; God, in Your abounding kindness, answer me with Your true deliverance.

Adon Olöm... **For Levels:** Ⓑ Ⓒ אֲדוֹן עוֹלָם ...

Adon olöm asher mölach,	אֲדוֹן עוֹלָם אֲשֶׁר מָלַךְ,
b'terem köl y'tzur nivrö.	בְּטֶרֶם כָּל יְצוּר נִבְרָא:
L'ays na-aso v'chef-tzo kol,	לְעֵת נַעֲשָׂה בְחֶפְצוֹ כֹּל,
azai melech sh'mo nikrö.	אֲזַי מֶלֶךְ שְׁמוֹ נִקְרָא:
V'acharei kichlos hakol, l'vado	וְאַחֲרֵי כִּכְלוֹת הַכֹּל, לְבַדּוֹ

yim-loch norö. V'hu höyöh	יִמְלֹךְ נוֹרָא : וְהוּא הָיָה וְהוּא
v'hu hoveh, v'hu yih-yeh	הֹוֶה, וְהוּא יִהְיֶה בְּתִפְאָרָה :
b'sif-öröh. V'hu echöd v'ayn	וְהוּא אֶחָד וְאֵין שֵׁנִי,
shayni, l'hamshil lo l'hach-biro.	לְהַמְשִׁיל לוֹ לְהַחְבִּירָה :
B'li rayshis b'li sachlis,	בְּלִי רֵאשִׁית בְּלִי תַכְלִית,
v'lo hö-oz v'hamisröh. V'hu	וְלוֹ הָעֹז וְהַמִּשְׂרָה : וְהוּא
ayli v'chai go-ali, v'tzur chevli	אֵלִי וְחַי גּוֹאֲלִי, וְצוּר חֶבְלִי
b'ays tzöröh. V'hu nisi umönos	בְּעֵת צָרָה : וְהוּא נִסִּי
li, m'nös kosi b'yom ekrö.	וּמָנוֹס לִי, מְנָת כּוֹסִי בְּיוֹם
B'yödo afkid ruchi,	אֶקְרָא : בְּיָדוֹ אַפְקִיד רוּחִי,
b'ays ishan v'ö-iröh. V'im	בְּעֵת אִישָׁן וְאָעִירָה : וְעִם
ruchi g'vi-yösi, adonöy li	רוּחִי גְּוִיָּתִי, יְיָ לִי
v'lo irö.	וְלֹא אִירָא :

Lord of the universe, who reigned before anything was created. He was, He is, and He shall be in glory. He is one, and there is no other to compare to Him, to consort with Him. Without beginning, without end, power and dominion belong to Him. Into His hand I entrust my spirit, when I sleep and when I wake. And with my soul, my body too, the Lord is with me.

Hö-aderes...   **For Levels:**   הָאַדֶּרֶת...
                                  ⓒ

Hö-aderes v'hö-emunöh,	הָאַדֶּרֶת וְהָאֱמוּנָה,
l'chai olömim.	לְחַי עוֹלָמִים:
Ha-binöh v'ha-b'röchöh,	הַבִּינָה וְהַבְּרָכָה,
l'chai olömim.	לְחַי עוֹלָמִים:
Ha-ga-avöh v'hag'dulöh,	הַגַּאֲוָה וְהַגְּדֻלָּה,
l'chai olömim.	לְחַי עוֹלָמִים:
Ha-day-öh v'hadibur,	הַדֵּעָה וְהַדִּבּוּר,
l'chai olömim.	לְחַי עוֹלָמִים:
Ha-hod v'he-hödör,	הַהוֹד וְהֶהָדָר,
l'chai olömim.	לְחַי עוֹלָמִים:
Ha-va-ad v'ha-vösikus,	הַוַּעַד וְהַוָּתִיקוּת,
l'chai olömim.	לְחַי עוֹלָמִים:
Ha-ziv v'ha-zohar,	הַזִּיו וְהַזֹּהַר,
l'chai olömim.	לְחַי עוֹלָמִים:
Ha-cha-yil v'ha-cho-sen,	הַחַיִל וְהַחֹסֶן,

Ha-teches v'ha-tohar,	הַטֶּכֶס וְהַטֹּהַר,
l'chai olömim.	לְחַי עוֹלָמִים:
Ha-yichud v'ha-yir-öh,	הַיִּחוּד וְהַיִּרְאָה,
l'chai olömim.	לְחַי עוֹלָמִים:
Ha-keser v'ha-kövod,	הַכֶּתֶר וְהַכָּבוֹד,
l'chai olömim.	לְחַי עוֹלָמִים:
Ha-lekach v'ha-libuv,	הַלֶּקַח וְהַלִּבּוּב,
l'chai olömim.	לְחַי עוֹלָמִים:
Ha-m'luchöh v'ha-memshölöh,	הַמְּלוּכָה וְהַמֶּמְשָׁלָה,
l'chai olömim.	לְחַי עוֹלָמִים:
Ha-noy v'ha-naytzach,	הַנּוֹי וְהַנֵּצַח,
l'chai olömim.	לְחַי עוֹלָמִים:
Ha-siguy v'hasegev,	הַסִּגּוּי וְהַסֶּגֶב,
l'chai olömim.	לְחַי עוֹלָמִים:
Hö-oz v'hö-anövöh,	הָעֹז וְהָעֲנָוָה,
l'chai olömim.	לְחַי עוֹלָמִים:
Ha-p'dus v'ha-p'ayr,	הַפְּדוּת וְהַפְּאֵר,
l'chai olömim.	לְחַי עוֹלָמִים:

Ha-tz'vi v'ha-tzedek,	הַצְּבִי וְהַצֶּדֶק,
l'chai olömim.	לְחַי עוֹלָמִים:
Ha-k'ri-öh v'ha-k'dushöh,	הַקְּרִיאָה וְהַקְּדֻשָּׁה,
l'chai olömim.	לְחַי עוֹלָמִים:
Hö-ron v'höro-maymos,	הָרוֹן וְהָרוֹמֵמוֹת
l'chai olömim.	לְחַי עוֹלָמִים:
Ha-shir v'ha-shevach,	הַשִּׁיר וְהַשֶּׁבַח,
l'chai olömim.	לְחַי עוֹלָמִים:
Ha-t'hilöh v'ha-tif-eres,	הַתְּהִלָּה וְהַתִּפְאֶרֶת,
l'chai olömim.	לְחַי עוֹלָמִים:

According to our Sages, this hymn is recited by the angels in heaven while singing the praises of God. The general meaning of this hymn is that all the attributes that can be enumerated are true only when applied to God. But when they are applied to mortal human beings, they cannot be true, because a human being has a limited life on earth and all his qualities are necessarily limited and imperfect.

Böruch She-ömar...	**For Levels:** Ⓑ Ⓒ	בָּרוּךְ שֶׁאָמַר...

Boys hold the front two Tzitzis while reciting this blessing, and kiss them at the end. This blessing is recited while standing.

85

L'shaym yichud kud-shö b'rich
לְשֵׁם יִחוּד קוּדְשָׁא בְּרִיךְ

hu ush'chintay l'yachadö shaym
הוּא וּשְׁכִינְתֵּהּ לְיַחֲדָא שֵׁם

yud kay b'vöv kay
"יוּד קֵי בְּוָו קֵי" (י"ה בו"ה)

b'yichudö sh'lim b'shaym
בְּיִחוּדָא שְׁלִים בְּשֵׁם

köl yisrö-ayl.
כָּל יִשְׂרָאֵל :

Böruch she-ömar v'hö-yöh
בָּרוּךְ שֶׁאָמַר וְהָיָה

hö-olöm, böruch hu,
הָעוֹלָם, בָּרוּךְ הוּא,

böruch omayr v'oseh,
בָּרוּךְ אוֹמֵר וְעוֹשֶׂה,

böruch gozayr um'ka-yaym,
בָּרוּךְ גּוֹזֵר וּמְקַיֵּם,

böruch oseh v'rayshis,
בָּרוּךְ עוֹשֶׂה בְרֵאשִׁית,

böruch m'ra-chaym al hö-öretz,
בָּרוּךְ מְרַחֵם עַל הָאָרֶץ,

böruch m'ra-chaym al
בָּרוּךְ מְרַחֵם עַל

ha-b'riyos, böruch m'shalaym
הַבְּרִיּוֹת, בָּרוּךְ מְשַׁלֵּם

söchör tov liray-öv, böruch
שָׂכָר טוֹב לִירֵאָיו, בָּרוּךְ

chai lö-ad v'kayöm lö-ne-tzach,
חַי לָעַד וְקַיָּם לָנֶצַח,

böruch podeh umatzil,
בָּרוּךְ פּוֹדֶה וּמַצִּיל,

böruch sh'mo. Böruch atöh
בָּרוּךְ שְׁמוֹ : בָּרוּךְ אַתָּה

adonöy elohaynu melech
יְיָ אֱלֹהֵינוּ מֶלֶךְ

hö-olöm, hö-ayl, öv	הָעוֹלָם, הָאֵל, אָב
höra-chamön, ha-m'hulöl	הָרַחֲמָן, הַמְהֻלָּל
b'feh amo, m'shuböch	בְּפֶה עַמּוֹ, מְשֻׁבָּח
um'fo-ör bil'shon chasidöv	וּמְפֹאָר בִּלְשׁוֹן חֲסִידָיו
va-avödöv, uv'shi-ray dövid	וַעֲבָדָיו, וּבְשִׁירֵי דָוִד
av-dechö. N'ha-lel'chö adonöy	עַבְדֶּךָ. נְהַלֶּלְךָ יְיָ
elohaynu, bish'vöchos	אֱלֹהֵינוּ, בִּשְׁבָחוֹת
uviz'miros. N'gadel'chö	וּבִזְמִרוֹת, נְגַדֶּלְךָ
un'shabay-chachö un'fö-er'chö,	וּנְשַׁבֵּחֲךָ וּנְפָאֶרְךָ,
v'namlich'chö v'nazkir	וְנַמְלִיכְךָ וְנַזְכִּיר
shim'chö malkaynu elohaynu,	שִׁמְךָ מַלְכֵּנוּ אֱלֹהֵינוּ.
yöchid, chay hö-olömim,	יָחִיד, חֵי הָעוֹלָמִים,
melech. M'shuböch um'fo-ör,	מֶלֶךְ. מְשֻׁבָּח וּמְפֹאָר
aday ad sh'mo ha-gödol.	עֲדֵי עַד שְׁמוֹ הַגָּדוֹל:
Böruch atöh adonöy, melech	בָּרוּךְ אַתָּה יְיָ, מֶלֶךְ
m'hulöl ba-tish-böchos.	מְהֻלָּל בַּתִּשְׁבָּחוֹת:

This blessing continues the theme of gratitude. We describe God's different manners to become more aware of Him, in order to praise Him more wholeheartedly in the following Psalms.

Ashrei...

For Levels:
(A) B C

אַשְׁרֵי ...

Ash-ray yosh'vay vaysechö,	אַשְׁרֵי יוֹשְׁבֵי בֵיתֶךָ,
od y'ha-l'luchö selöh.	עוֹד יְהַלְלוּךְ סֶּלָה:
Ash-ray hö-öm sheköchö lo,	אַשְׁרֵי הָעָם שֶׁכָּכָה לּוֹ,
ash-ray hö-öm she-adonöy	אַשְׁרֵי הָעָם שֶׁיְיָ
elohöv. T'hilöh l'dövid,	אֱלֹהָיו: תְּהִלָּה לְדָוִד,
aro-mim'chö elohai ha-melech,	אֲרוֹמִמְךָ אֱלוֹהַי הַמֶּלֶךְ,
va-avö-r'chöh shim'chö l'olöm	וַאֲבָרְכָה שִׁמְךָ לְעוֹלָם
vö-ed. B'chöl yom avö-r'chekö,	וָעֶד: בְּכָל יוֹם אֲבָרְכֶךָ,
va-aha-l'löh shim'chö l'olöm	וַאֲהַלְלָה שִׁמְךָ לְעוֹלָם
vö-ed. Gödol adonöy um'hulöl	וָעֶד: גָּדוֹל יְיָ וּמְהֻלָּל
m'od, v'lig'dulöso ayn chayker.	מְאֹד, וְלִגְדֻלָּתוֹ אֵין חֵקֶר:
Dor l'dor y'shabach ma-aschö,	דּוֹר לְדוֹר יְשַׁבַּח מַעֲשֶׂיךָ,
ug'vuroschö yagidu. Hadar	וּגְבוּרֹתֶיךָ יַגִּידוּ: הֲדַר
k'vod hodechö, v'div'ray	כְּבוֹד הוֹדֶךָ, וְדִבְרֵי
nif-l'osechö ö-sichöh. Ve-ezuz	נִפְלְאֹתֶיךָ אָשִׂיחָה: וֶעֱזוּז

88

no-r'osechö yomayru,	נוֹרְאֹתֶיךָ יֹאמֵרוּ,
ug'dulös'chö asap'renöh.	וּגְדֻלָּתְךָ אֲסַפְּרֶנָּה:
Zecher rav tuv'chö yabi-u,	זֵכֶר רַב טוּבְךָ יַבִּיעוּ,
v'tzid'kös'chö y'ra-naynu.	וְצִדְקָתְךָ יְרַנֵּנוּ:
Chanun v'rachum adonöy,	חַנּוּן וְרַחוּם יְיָ,
erech apa-yim ug'döl chösed.	אֶרֶךְ אַפַּיִם וּגְדָל חָסֶד:
Tov adonöy lakol, v'ra-chamöv	טוֹב יְיָ לַכֹּל, וְרַחֲמָיו
al köl ma-asöv. Yoduchö	עַל כָּל מַעֲשָׂיו: יוֹדוּךָ
adonöy köl ma-a-sechö,	יְיָ כָּל מַעֲשֶׂיךָ,
va-chasi-dechö y'vör-chuchöh.	וַחֲסִידֶיךָ יְבָרְכוּכָה:
K'vod mal'chus'chö yomayru,	כְּבוֹד מַלְכוּתְךָ יֹאמֵרוּ,
ug'vurö-s'chö y'da-bayru.	וּגְבוּרָתְךָ יְדַבֵּרוּ:
L'hodi-ah liv'nay hö-ödöm	לְהוֹדִיעַ לִבְנֵי הָאָדָם
g'vurosöv, uch'vod hadar	גְּבוּרֹתָיו, וּכְבוֹד הֲדַר
mal'chuso. Mal'chus'chö,	מַלְכוּתוֹ: מַלְכוּתְךָ
mal'chus köl olömim,	מַלְכוּת כָּל עוֹלָמִים,
umem-shal-t'chö b'chöl dor	וּמֶמְשַׁלְתְּךָ בְּכָל דּוֹר
vödor. Somaych adonöy l'chöl	וָדֹר: סוֹמֵךְ יְיָ לְכָל

hanof'lim, v'zokayf l'chöl	הַנֹּפְלִים, וְזוֹקֵף לְכָל
hak'kufim. Aynay chol aylechö	הַכְּפוּפִים : עֵינֵי כֹל אֵלֶיךָ
y'sa-bayru, v'atöh nosayn löhem	יְשַׂבֵּרוּ, וְאַתָּה נוֹתֵן לָהֶם
es öchlöm b'ito. Posay-ach es	אֶת אָכְלָם בְּעִתּוֹ : פּוֹתֵחַ אֶת
yödechö, umasbi-a l'chöl chai	יָדֶךָ, וּמַשְׂבִּיעַ לְכָל חַי
rötzon. Tzadik adonöy b'chöl	רָצוֹן : צַדִּיק יְיָ בְּכָל
d'röchöv, v'chösid b'chöl	דְּרָכָיו, וְחָסִיד בְּכָל
ma-asöv. Körov adonöy l'chöl	מַעֲשָׂיו : קָרוֹב יְיָ לְכָל
ko-r'öv, l'chol asher yikrö-u-hu	קֹרְאָיו, לְכֹל אֲשֶׁר יִקְרָאֻהוּ
ve-emes. R'tzon y'ray-öv ya-aseh,	בֶאֱמֶת : רְצוֹן יְרֵאָיו יַעֲשֶׂה,
v'es shav-ösöm yishma	וְאֶת שַׁוְעָתָם יִשְׁמַע
v'yoshi-aym. Shomayr adonöy es	וְיוֹשִׁיעֵם : שׁוֹמֵר יְיָ אֶת
köl ohavöv, v'ays köl hör-shö-im	כָּל אֹהֲבָיו, וְאֵת כָּל הָרְשָׁעִים
yash-mid. T'hilas adonöy y'daber	יַשְׁמִיד : תְּהִלַּת יְיָ יְדַבֶּר
pi, vi-vöraych köl bösör shaym	פִּי, וִיבָרֵךְ כָּל בָּשָׂר שֵׁם
köd-sho l'olöm vö-ed.	קָדְשׁוֹ לְעוֹלָם וָעֶד :
Va-anachnu n'vöraych yöh,	וַאֲנַחְנוּ נְבָרֵךְ יָהּ,
may-atöh v'ad olöm ha-l'luyöh.	מֵעַתָּה וְעַד עוֹלָם, הַלְלוּיָהּ :

90

Our Sages tell us that whoever says *Ashrei* three times a day will have a share in the world to come. Indeed, it is part of the daily prayers so that by praying each day, we recite this Psalm three times. Each verse begins with a letter from the Hebrew alphabet (except the letter נ which is included in the next verse). This is to express that we praise God with all possible forms of expression.

Ha-l'luyöh...   **For Levels:**   ...הַלְלוּיָהּ

6

Ha-l'luyöh, ha-l'lu ayl	הַלְלוּיָהּ, הַלְלוּ אֵל
b'köd-sho, ha-l'luhu bir'kiah	בְּקָדְשׁוֹ, הַלְלוּהוּ בִּרְקִיעַ
uzo. Ha-l'luhu big'vurosöv,	עֻזּוֹ: הַלְלוּהוּ בִגְבוּרֹתָיו,
ha-l'luhu k'rov gud-lo.	הַלְלוּהוּ כְּרֹב גֻּדְלוֹ:
Ha-l'luhu b'sayka shoför,	הַלְלוּהוּ בְּתֵקַע שׁוֹפָר,
ha-l'luhu b'nayvel v'chinor.	הַלְלוּהוּ בְּנֵבֶל וְכִנּוֹר:
Ha-l'luhu b'sof umöchol,	הַלְלוּהוּ בְּתֹף וּמָחוֹל,
ha-l'luhu b'minim v'ugöv.	הַלְלוּהוּ בְּמִנִּים וְעֻגָב:
Ha-l'luhu b'tzil-tz'lay shöma,	הַלְלוּהוּ בְּצִלְצְלֵי שָׁמַע,
ha-l'luhu b'tzil-tz'lay s'ruöh.	הַלְלוּהוּ בְּצִלְצְלֵי תְרוּעָה:
Kol ha-n'shömöh t'halayl yöh	כֹּל הַנְּשָׁמָה תְּהַלֵּל יָהּ

ha-l'luyöh. Kol ha-n'shömöh   הַלְלוּיָהּ : כֹּל הַנְּשָׁמָה

t'halyl yöh ha-l'luyöh.   תְּהַלֵּל יָהּ הַלְלוּיָהּ :

In this final Psalm we glorify God with 13 expressions of glory. This is a befitting introduction to the culmination of our prayers in the Shema and the Amidah that follow.

Böruch...   **For Levels:**   בָּרוּך ...

G

Böruch adonöy l'olöm,   בָּרוּךְ יְיָ לְעוֹלָם,

ömayn v'ömayn. Böruch   אָמֵן וְאָמֵן. בָּרוּךְ

adonöy mitzi-yon shochayn   יְיָ מִצִּיּוֹן שֹׁכֵן

y'rushölö-yim, ha-l'luyöh.   יְרוּשָׁלָיִם, הַלְלוּיָהּ :

Böruch adonöy elohim elohay   בָּרוּךְ יְיָ אֱלֹהִים אֱלֹהֵי

yisrö-ayl osay niflö-os   יִשְׂרָאֵל, עֹשֵׂה נִפְלָאוֹת

l'vado. Uvöruch shaym k'vodo   לְבַדּוֹ : וּבָרוּךְ שֵׁם כְּבוֹדוֹ

l'olöm, v'yimölay ch'vodo es   לְעוֹלָם, וְיִמָּלֵא כְבוֹדוֹ אֶת

köl hö-öretz, ömayn v'ömayn.   כָּל הָאָרֶץ, אָמֵן וְאָמֵן.

This prayer begns the final sections of the Verses of Praise portion of our morning prayers. We rise for this prayer and remain standing for the next few passages, emphasizing their importance, and to follow the example of

King David and the prophet Nehemiah who were standing out of honor when they recited it as well.

Yishtabach...

For Levels:
Ⓑ Ⓒ

יִשְׁתַּבַּח ...

Uv'chayn yishtabach shim'chö	וּבְכֵן יִשְׁתַּבַּח שִׁמְךָ
lö-ad malkaynu, hö-ayl,	לָעַד מַלְכֵּנוּ, הָאֵל,
ha-melech, ha-gödol	הַמֶּלֶךְ הַגָּדוֹל
v'haködosh, ba-shöma-yim	וְהַקָּדוֹשׁ בַּשָּׁמַיִם
uvö-öretz. Ki l'chö nö-eh	וּבָאָרֶץ. כִּי לְךָ נָאֶה
adonöy elohay-nu vay-lohay	יְיָ אֱלֹהֵינוּ וֵאלֹהֵי
avosaynu l'olöm vö-ed. Shir	אֲבוֹתֵינוּ לְעוֹלָם וָעֶד: שִׁיר
ush'vöchöh, ha-layl v'zimröh,	וּשְׁבָחָה, הַלֵּל וְזִמְרָה,
oz umemshölöh, ne-tzach,	עֹז וּמֶמְשָׁלָה, נֶצַח,
g'dulöh ug'vuröh, t'hilöh	גְּדֻלָּה וּגְבוּרָה, תְּהִלָּה
v'sif-eres, k'dushö umal'chus.	וְתִפְאֶרֶת, קְדֻשָּׁה וּמַלְכוּת:
B'röchos v'hodö-os, l'shim'chö	בְּרָכוֹת וְהוֹדָאוֹת לְשִׁמְךָ
ha-gödol v'ha-ködosh	הַגָּדוֹל וְהַקָּדוֹשׁ,

93

umay-olöm ad olöm, atöh	וּמֵעוֹלָם עַד עוֹלָם אַתָּה
ayl. Böruch atöh adonöy, ayl	אֵל. בָּרוּךְ אַתָּה יְיָ, אֵל
melech, gödol um'hulöl	מֶלֶךְ גָּדוֹל וּמְהֻלָּל
batish-böchos, ayl ha-hodö-os,	בַּתִּשְׁבָּחוֹת, אֵל הַהוֹדָאוֹת,
adon ha-niflö-os, boray köl	אֲדוֹן הַנִּפְלָאוֹת, בּוֹרֵא כָּל
ha-n'shömos, ribon köl	הַנְּשָׁמוֹת, רִבּוֹן כָּל
ha-ma-asim, ha-bochayr	הַמַּעֲשִׂים, הַבּוֹחֵר
b'shiray zimröh, melch yöchid	בְּשִׁירֵי זִמְרָה, מֶלֶךְ יָחִיד
chay hö-olömim.	חֵי הָעוֹלָמִים :

The Leader says:	חזן :
Bör'chu es adonöy	בָּרְכוּ אֶת יְיָ
ha-m'voröch.	הַמְבֹרָךְ :
Congregation, then leader:	קהל וחזן :
Böruch adonöy ha-m'voröch	בָּרוּךְ יְיָ הַמְבֹרָךְ
l'olöm vö-ed.	לְעוֹלָם וָעֶד :

Yotzayr Or...

For Levels:
B C

יוֹצֵר אוֹר ...

Böruch atöh adonöy elohaynu
melech hö-olöm, yo-tzayr
or uvoray cho-shech, oseh
shölom uvoray es hakol.

בָּרוּךְ אַתָּה יְיָ,
אֱלֹהֵינוּ מֶלֶךְ הָעוֹלָם, יוֹצֵר
אוֹר וּבוֹרֵא חֹשֶׁךְ, עוֹשֶׂה
שָׁלוֹם וּבוֹרֵא אֶת הַכֹּל:

This is the first blessing before the Shema. With this blessing we acknowledge the awesome change from day to night. What may seem a 'natural' and 'ordinary' change from day to night, from night to day, from summer to winter, from winter to summer, and so on, is really a wonderful act of Creation by God.

Ayl Ödon...

For Levels:
B C

אֵל אָדוֹן ...

Ayl ödon al köl ha-ma-asim,
böruch um'voröch b'fi köl
ha-n'shömöh, göd-lo v'tuvo
mölay olöm, da-as us'vunöh
sov'vim hodo. Ha-mis-gö-eh al

אֵל אָדוֹן עַל כָּל הַמַּעֲשִׂים,
בָּרוּךְ וּמְבוֹרָךְ בְּפִי כָּל
הַנְּשָׁמָה, גָּדְלוֹ וְטוּבוֹ
מָלֵא עוֹלָם, דַּעַת וּתְבוּנָה
סוֹבְבִים הוֹדוֹ: הַמִּתְגָּאֶה עַל

95

cha-yos ha-kodesh, v'neh-dör	חַיּוֹת הַקֹּדֶשׁ, וְנֶהְדָּר
b'chövod al ha-merkövöh,	בְּכָבוֹד עַל הַמֶּרְכָּבָה,
z'chus umishor lif'nay chis-o,	זְכוּת וּמִישׁוֹר לִפְנֵי כִסְאוֹ,
chesed v'rachamim mölay	חֶסֶד וְרַחֲמִים מָלֵא
ch'vodo. Tovim m'oros,	כְבוֹדוֹ: טוֹבִים מְאוֹרוֹת
shebörö elohaynu, y'tzöröm	שֶׁבָּרָא אֱלֹהֵינוּ, יְצָרָם
b'da-as b'vinoh uv'haskayl,	בְּדַעַת בְּבִינָה וּבְהַשְׂכֵּל,
ko-ach ug'vuröh nösan	כֹּחַ וּגְבוּרָה נָתַן
böhem, lih-yos mosh'lim	בָּהֶם, לִהְיוֹת מוֹשְׁלִים
b'kerev tay-vayl. M'lay-im ziv	בְּקֶרֶב תֵּבֵל: מְלֵאִים זִיו
um'fikim nogah, nö-eh zivom	וּמְפִיקִים נֹגַהּ, נָאֶה זִיוָם
b'chöl hö-olöm, s'maychim	בְּכָל הָעוֹלָם, שְׂמֵחִים
b'tzaysöm v'sösim b'vo-öm,	בְּצֵאתָם וְשָׂשִׂים בְּבוֹאָם,
osim b'aymöh r'tzon konöm.	עוֹשִׂים בְּאֵימָה רְצוֹן קוֹנָם:
P'ayr v'chövod nos'nim	פְּאֵר וְכָבוֹד נוֹתְנִים
lish'mo, tzö-hölöh v'rinöh	לִשְׁמוֹ, צָהֳלָה וְרִנָּה
l'zaycher mal'chuso, körö	לְזֵכֶר מַלְכוּתוֹ, קָרָא
la-shemesh va-yizrach or, rö-öh	לַשֶּׁמֶשׁ וַיִּזְרַח אוֹר, רָאָה

v'hiskin tzuras hal'vönöh. וְהִתְקִין צוּרַת הַלְּבָנָה:

Shevach nos'nim lo köl tz'vö שֶׁבַח נוֹתְנִים לוֹ כָּל צְבָא

mörom, tif-eres ug'dulöh, מָרוֹם, תִּפְאֶרֶת וּגְדֻלָּה,

s'röfim v'cha-yos שְׂרָפִים וְחַיּוֹת

v'ofa-nay ha-kodesh. וְאוֹפַנֵּי הַקֹּדֶשׁ:

This is a prayer-poem written in alphabetical order, offering more praise to God, the Master of all creatures. It was composed alphabetically to illustrate that the world was created by the word of God and for the sake of the Torah, written in the twenty-two letters of the Hebrew alphabet.

Es Shaym...   **For Levels:** 6   אֶת שֵׁם...

Es shaym hö-ayl, ha-melech אֶת שֵׁם הָאֵל, הַמֶּלֶךְ

ha-gödol, ha-gibor v'ha-noröh, הַגָּדוֹל, הַגִּבּוֹר וְהַנּוֹרָא,

ködosh hu. V'chulöm m'kab'lim קָדוֹשׁ הוּא: וְכֻלָּם מְקַבְּלִים

a-layhem ol mal'chus shöma-yim עֲלֵיהֶם עֹל מַלְכוּת שָׁמַיִם

zeh mi-zeh, v'nos'nim b'ahavöh זֶה מִזֶּה, וְנוֹתְנִים בְּאַהֲבָה

r'shus zeh lözeh, l'hakdish רְשׁוּת זֶה לָזֶה, לְהַקְדִּישׁ

l'yo-tz'rom b'nachas ru-ach, לְיוֹצְרָם בְּנַחַת רוּחַ,

b'söföh v'ruröh uvin'imöh	בְּשָׂפָה בְרוּרָה וּבִנְעִימָה
k'doshöh. Kulöm k'echöd onim	קְדוֹשָׁה: כֻּלָם כְּאֶחָד עוֹנִים
b'ay-möh v'om'rim b'yir-öh.	בְּאֵימָה וְאוֹמְרִים בְּיִרְאָה:
Ködosh, ködosh ködosh,	קָדוֹשׁ, קָדוֹשׁ, קָדוֹשׁ,
adonöy tz'vö-os, m'lo chöl	יְיָ צְבָאוֹת, מְלֹא כָל
hö-öretz k'vodo. V'hö-ofanim	הָאָרֶץ כְּבוֹדוֹ: וְהָאוֹפַנִּים
v'cha-yos ha-kodesh b'ra-ash	וְחַיּוֹת הַקֹּדֶשׁ בְּרַעַשׁ
gödol mis-na-s'im l'umas	גָּדוֹל מִתְנַשְׂאִים לְעֻמַּת
ha-s'röfim, l'umösöm	הַשְּׂרָפִים, לְעֻמָּתָם
m'shab'chim v'om'rim. Böruch	מְשַׁבְּחִים וְאוֹמְרִים: בָּרוּךְ
k'vod adonöy mim'komo.	כְּבוֹד יְיָ מִמְּקוֹמוֹ:

Here we have a prayer uttered by the angels, who proclaim God's praise with a mighty sound. *Kadosh* means "separate;" to say that God is holy is to say that God is separated from, and unaffected by, the world He created.

Löayl Böruch...   **For Levels:** 6   לָאֵל בָּרוּךְ...

Löayl böruch n'imos	לָאֵל בָּרוּךְ נְעִימוֹת
yi-taynu, lö-melech ayl chai	יִתֵּנוּ, לַמֶּלֶךְ אֵל חַי

98

v'ka-yöm, z'miros yomay-ru
v'sish-böchos yash-mi-u,
ki hu l'vado mörom v'ködosh,
po-ayl g'vuros, oseh
chadöshos, ba-al milchömos,
zoray-a tz'dökos, matzmi-ach
y'shu-os, boray r'fu-os,
norö s'hilos, adon
ha-niflö-os, ha-m'chadaysh
b'tuvo b'chöl yom tömid
ma-asay v'rayshis. Kö-ömur,
l'osay orim g'dolim, ki
l'olöm chasdo. Böruch atöh
adonöy, yo-tzayr ha-m'oros.

וְקַיָּם, זְמִירוֹת יֹאמֵרוּ
וְתִשְׁבָּחוֹת יַשְׁמִיעוּ, כִּי
הוּא לְבַדּוֹ מָרוֹם וְקָדוֹשׁ,
פּוֹעֵל גְּבוּרוֹת, עוֹשֶׂה
חֲדָשׁוֹת, בַּעַל מִלְחָמוֹת,
זוֹרֵעַ צְדָקוֹת, מַצְמִיחַ
יְשׁוּעוֹת, בּוֹרֵא רְפוּאוֹת,
נוֹרָא תְהִלּוֹת, אֲדוֹן
הַנִּפְלָאוֹת, הַמְחַדֵּשׁ
בְּטוּבוֹ בְּכָל יוֹם תָּמִיד
מַעֲשֵׂה בְרֵאשִׁית: כָּאָמוּר,
לְעֹשֵׂה אוֹרִים גְּדֹלִים, כִּי
לְעוֹלָם חַסְדּוֹ: בָּרוּךְ אַתָּה
יְיָ, יוֹצֵר הַמְּאוֹרוֹת:

This is the last section of the first blessing before the Shema. This blessing begins and concludes with the idea that God has never stopped for a moment the process of creation. We bless God as the creator of the "luminaries." Here we have in mind not only the physical lights, the light of the sun and moon and other forms of illumination, but also "lights" in a deeper sense, the light of the Torah and its mitzvot.

Sh'ma Yisrö-ayl...   **For Levels:**   שְׁמַע יִשְׂרָאֵל ...
🄰 🄱 🄲

The Shema is the essence of our faith. It consists of three paragraphs taken from the Torah (Bible). The first paragraph begins with the statement: "The Lord is One." It goes on to tell us that we must love God and dedicate our lives to carrying out His will. This section also contains the two mitzvot of Tefillin and Mezuzah, which remind us that we are Jews.

The second chapter contains a promise that if we fulfill and observe God's commands we shall be a happy people in our land. If not, we will suffer exile and hardships in strange lands, so that by suffering and trouble we will learn the ways of God and return to Him.

The third chapter contains the commandment of Tzitzit, the distinctive Jewish garment which is a constant reminder of all the precepts of the Torah. We are reminded, also, that God brought us out of Egypt and made us His people, and that we accepted Him as our God.

Man and boys gather their four Tzitzit in the left hand. It is customary to cover the eyes with our right hand while reciting the first verse of the Shema, to increase concentration.

Sh'ma yisrö-ayl, adonöy   שְׁמַע יִשְׂרָאֵל, יְיָ

elohaynu, adonöy echöd.   אֱלֹהֵינוּ, יְיָ אֶחָד :

Hear, O Israel, the Lord is our God, the Lord is One.

Remove your hand from your eyes, and say the following in an undertone:

Böruch shaym k'vod
mal'chuso l'olöm vö-ed.

בָּרוּךְ שֵׁם כְּבוֹד
מַלְכוּתוֹ לְעוֹלָם וָעֶד:

Blessed be the name of the glory of His kingdom forever and ever.

Continue in a regular tone below:

V'öhavtö ays adonöy elohechö,
b'chöl l'vöv'chö, uv'chöl
naf-sh'chö, uv'chöl m'odechö.
V'hö-yu ha-d'vörim hö-ay-leh
asher önochi m'tzav'chö
ha-yom, al l'vö-vechö.
V'shinan-töm l'vö-nechö
v'dibartö böm, b'shiv-t'chö
b'vaysechö, uv'lech-t'chö
vaderech, uv'shöch-b'chö,
uv'kumechö. Uk'shartöm l'os
al yödechö, v'hö-yu l'totöfos
bayn aynechö. Uch'savtöm

וְאָהַבְתָּ אֵת יְיָ אֱלֹהֶיךָ,
בְּכָל לְבָבְךָ, וּבְכָל
נַפְשְׁךָ, וּבְכָל מְאֹדֶךָ:
וְהָיוּ הַדְּבָרִים הָאֵלֶּה
אֲשֶׁר אָנֹכִי מְצַוְּךָ
הַיּוֹם, עַל לְבָבֶךָ:
וְשִׁנַּנְתָּם לְבָנֶיךָ
וְדִבַּרְתָּ בָּם, בְּשִׁבְתְּךָ
בְּבֵיתֶךָ, וּבְלֶכְתְּךָ
בַדֶּרֶךְ, וּבְשָׁכְבְּךָ,
וּבְקוּמֶךָ: וּקְשַׁרְתָּם לְאוֹת
עַל יָדֶךָ, וְהָיוּ לְטֹטָפֹת
בֵּין עֵינֶיךָ: וּכְתַבְתָּם

101

al m'zuzos bay-sechö, עַל מְזֻזוֹת בֵּיתֶךָ,
uvish'örechö. וּבִשְׁעָרֶיךָ:

You shall love the Lord your God with all your heart, with all your soul, and with all your might. And these words which I command you today shall be upon your heart. You shall teach them thoroughly to your children, and you shall speak of them when you sit in your house and when you walk on the road, when you lie down and when you rise. You shall bind them as a sign upon your hand, and they shall be for a reminder between your eyes. And you shall write them upon the doorposts of your house and upon your gates.

Levels Ⓑ Ⓒ continue below:

V'hö-yöh im shömo-a tish-m'u וְהָיָה אִם שָׁמֹעַ תִּשְׁמְעוּ
el mitzvo-sai asher önochi אֶל מִצְוֹתַי אֲשֶׁר אָנֹכִי
m'tza-veh es'chem ha-yom, מְצַוֶּה אֶתְכֶם הַיּוֹם,
l'ahavöh es adonöy לְאַהֲבָה אֶת יְיָ
elohaychem ul'öv'do, b'chöl אֱלֹהֵיכֶם וּלְעָבְדוֹ, בְּכָל
l'vav'chem uv'chöl לְבַבְכֶם וּבְכָל
naf-sh'chem. V'nösati m'tar נַפְשְׁכֶם: וְנָתַתִּי מְטַר
ar-tz'chem b'ito yo-reh אַרְצְכֶם בְּעִתּוֹ יוֹרֶה
umalkosh, v'ösaftö d'gönechö וּמַלְקוֹשׁ, וְאָסַפְתָּ דְגָנֶךָ

102

v'sirosh'chö v'yitz-hörechö.	וְתִירשְׁךָ וְיִצְהָרֶךָ:
V'nösati aysev b'söd'chö	וְנָתַתִּי עֵשֶׂב בְּשָׂדְךָ
liv'hemtechö, v'öchaltö	לִבְהֶמְתֶּךָ, וְאָכַלְתָּ
v'sövö-tö. Hishöm'ru löchem	וְשָׂבָעְתָּ: הִשָּׁמְרוּ לָכֶם
pen yifteh l'vav'chem, v'sartem	פֶּן יִפְתֶּה לְבַבְכֶם, וְסַרְתֶּם
va-avad-tem elohim achayrim	וַעֲבַדְתֶּם אֱלֹהִים אֲחֵרִים
v'hish-tachavisem löhem.	וְהִשְׁתַּחֲוִיתֶם לָהֶם:
V'chöröh af adonöy böchem	וְחָרָה אַף יְיָ בָּכֶם
v'ötzar es ha-shöma-yim v'lo	וְעָצַר אֶת הַשָּׁמַיִם וְלֹא
yih-yeh mötör v'hö-adömöh lo	יִהְיֶה מָטָר וְהָאֲדָמָה לֹא
sitayn es y'vulöh, va-avad-tem	תִתֵּן אֶת יְבוּלָהּ וַאֲבַדְתֶּם
m'hayröh may-al hö-öretz	מְהֵרָה מֵעַל הָאָרֶץ
ha-tovöh asher adonöy nosayn	הַטֹּבָה אֲשֶׁר יְיָ נֹתֵן
löchem. V'samtem es d'vörai	לָכֶם: וְשַׂמְתֶּם אֶת דְּבָרַי
ayleh al l'vav'chem v'al	אֵלֶּה עַל לְבַבְכֶם וְעַל
naf-sh'chem uk'shartem osöm	נַפְשְׁכֶם וּקְשַׁרְתֶּם אֹתָם
l'os al yed'chem v'hö-yu	לְאוֹת עַל יֶדְכֶם וְהָיוּ
l'totöfos bayn ay-naychem.	לְטוֹטָפֹת בֵּין עֵינֵיכֶם:

V'limad-tem osöm es	וְלִמַּדְתֶּם אֹתָם אֶת
b'naychem l'dabayr böm,	בְּנֵיכֶם לְדַבֵּר בָּם,
b'shiv-t'chö b'vaysechö	בְּשִׁבְתְּךָ בְּבֵיתֶךָ
uv'lech-t'chö va-derech	וּבְלֶכְתְּךָ בַדֶּרֶךְ
uv'shöch-b'chö uv'kumechö.	וּבְשָׁכְבְּךָ וּבְקוּמֶךָ :
Uch'savtöm al m'zuzos	וּכְתַבְתָּם עַל מְזוּזֹת
baysechö uvish'örechö.	בֵּיתֶךָ וּבִשְׁעָרֶיךָ :
L'ma-an yirbu y'maychem	לְמַעַן יִרְבּוּ יְמֵיכֶם
vimay v'naychem al	וִימֵי בְנֵיכֶם עַל
hö-adömöh asher nishba	הָאֲדָמָה אֲשֶׁר נִשְׁבַּע
adonöy la-avosaychem lösays	יְיָ לַאֲבֹתֵיכֶם לָתֵת
löhem, kimay ha-shöma-yim	לָהֶם, כִּימֵי הַשָּׁמַיִם
al hö-öretz.	עַל הָאָרֶץ :

And it will be, if you will diligently obey My commandments which I enjoin upon you this day, to love the Lord your God and to serve Him with all your heart and with all your soul, I will give rain for your land at the proper time, the early rain and the late rain, and you will gather in your grain, your wine and your oil. And I will give grass in your fields for your cattle, and you will eat and be sated. Take care lest your heart be lured away, and you turn astray and worship alien gods and bow down to them. For then the Lord's wrath will flare up against you, and He will close the heavens so that there will be no rain and the

earth will not yield its produce, and you will swiftly perish from the good land which the Lord gives you. Therefore, place these words of Mine upon your heart and upon your soul, and bind them for a sign on your hand, and they shall be for a reminder between your eyes. You shall teach them to your children, to speak of them when you sit in your house and when you walk on the road, when you lie down and when you rise. And you shall inscribe them on the doorposts of your house and on your gates — so that your days and the days of your children may be prolonged on the land which the Lord swore to your fathers to give to them for as long as the heavens are above the earth.

Men and boys hold their tzitzit in the right and and kiss them whenever saying the word *Tzitzis* in the following paragraph:

Va-yomer adonöy el mosheh	וַיֹּאמֶר יְיָ אֶל מֹשֶׁה
laymor. Dabayr el b'nay	לֵּאמֹר: דַּבֵּר אֶל בְּנֵי
yisrö-ayl v'ömartö alay-hem	יִשְׂרָאֵל וְאָמַרְתָּ אֲלֵהֶם
v'östu löhem tzitzis al	וְעָשׂוּ לָהֶם צִיצִת עַל
kan'fay vig'dayhem l'dorosöm,	כַּנְפֵי בִגְדֵיהֶם לְדֹרֹתָם,
v'nös'nu al tzitzis ha-könöf,	וְנָתְנוּ עַל צִיצִת הַכָּנָף,
p'sil t'chayles. V'hö-yöh	פְּתִיל תְּכֵלֶת: וְהָיָה
löchem l'tzitzis, ur'isem oso	לָכֶם לְצִיצִת, וּרְאִיתֶם אֹתוֹ
uz'chartem es köl mitzvos	וּזְכַרְתֶּם אֶת כָּל מִצְוֹת
adonöy va-asisem osöm, v'lo	יְיָ וַעֲשִׂיתֶם אֹתָם, וְלֹא

105

sösuru acha-ray l'vav'chem	תָתוּרוּ אַחֲרֵי לְבַבְכֶם
v'acharay aynay-chem asher	וְאַחֲרֵי עֵינֵיכֶם אֲשֶׁר
atem zonim acha-rayhem.	אַתֶּם זֹנִים אַחֲרֵיהֶם :
L'ma-an tiz-k'ru va-asisem es	לְמַעַן תִּזְכְּרוּ וַעֲשִׂיתֶם אֶת
köl mitzvo-söy, vih-yisem	כָּל מִצְוֹתָי, וִהְיִיתֶם
k'doshim laylo-haychem.	קְדֹשִׁים לֵאלֹהֵיכֶם :
Ani adonöy elo-haychem asher	אֲנִי יְיָ אֱלֹהֵיכֶם אֲשֶׁר
ho-tzaysi es'chem may-eretz	הוֹצֵאתִי אֶתְכֶם מֵאֶרֶץ
mitzra-yim lih-yos löchem	מִצְרַיִם לִהְיוֹת לָכֶם
laylohim, ani adonöy	לֵאלֹהִים, אֲנִי יְיָ
elo-haychem. Emes.	אֱלֹהֵיכֶם : אֱמֶת.

The Lord spoke to Moses, saying: Speak to the children of Israel and tell them to make for themselves fringes on the corners of their garments throughout their generations, and to attach a thread of blue on the fringe of each corner. They shall be to you as tzitzit, and you shall look upon them and remember all the commandments of the Lord and fulfill them, and you will not follow after your heart and after your eyes by which you go astray — so that you may remember and fulfill all My commandments and be holy to your God. I am the Lord your God who brought you out of the land of Egypt to be your God; I, the Lord, am your God. Truth...

V'ya-tziv...

For Levels:

6

וְיַצִּיב...

V'ya-tziv, v'nöchon, v'ka-yöm,	וְיַצִּיב, וְנָכוֹן, וְקַיָּם,
v'yöshör, v'ne-emön; v'öhuv	וְיָשָׁר, וְנֶאֱמָן; וְאָהוּב
v'chöviv, v'nechmöd v'nö-im,	וְחָבִיב, וְנֶחְמָד וְנָעִים,
v'norö v'adir, um'sukön,	וְנוֹרָא וְאַדִּיר, וּמְתֻקָּן,
um'kuböl, v'tov v'yöfeh,	וּמְקֻבָּל, וְטוֹב וְיָפֶה,
ha-dövör ha-zeh ölaynu l'olöm	הַדָּבָר הַזֶּה עָלֵינוּ לְעוֹלָם
vö-ed. Emes, elohay olöm	וָעֶד: אֱמֶת, אֱלֹהֵי עוֹלָם
malkaynu, tzur ya-akov	מַלְכֵּנוּ, צוּר יַעֲקֹב מָגֵן
mögayn yish-aynu, l'dor vödor	יִשְׁעֵנוּ, לְדוֹר וָדוֹר הוּא
hu ka-yöm, ush'mo ka-yöm,	קַיָּם, וּשְׁמוֹ קַיָּם,
v'chi-so nö-chon, umal'chuso	וְכִסְאוֹ נָכוֹן, וּמַלְכוּתוֹ
ve-emunöso lö-ad ka-yemes.	וֶאֱמוּנָתוֹ לָעַד קַיֶּמֶת:
Ud'vöröv chö-yim v'ka-yömim,	וּדְבָרָיו חָיִים וְקַיָּמִים,
ne-emönim v'neche-mödim	נֶאֱמָנִים וְנֶחֱמָדִים
lö-ad ul'öl'may olömim,	לָעַד וּלְעוֹלְמֵי עוֹלָמִים,

107

al avosaynu v'ölaynu, עַל אֲבוֹתֵינוּ וְעָלֵינוּ,

al bö-naynu v'al doro-saynu, עַל בָּנֵינוּ וְעַל דּוֹרוֹתֵינוּ,

v'al köl doros zera וְעַל כָּל דּוֹרוֹת זֶרַע

yisrö-ayl avödechö. יִשְׂרָאֵל עֲבָדֶיךָ:

This is a continuation of the theme of the blessing preceding the Shema. It begins a series of 16 words which are closely related to the concept of truth, emphasizing the truthfulness of all that we declared in the Shema. The 16 expressions are said to refer to the 16 verses in the first two sections of the Shema. This prayer speaks of God's eternal faithfulness to the Jewish people, of the great love which he has shown to us throughout the ages, by liberating our ancestors from Egypt, and continuing to be our "Shield of deliverance" in the most difficult of times.

Shirö Chadöshö...   **For Levels:** ℬ 𝒞   שִׁירָה חֲדָשָׁה...

Shirö cha-döshöh shib'chu שִׁירָה חֲדָשָׁה שִׁבְּחוּ

g'u-lim l'shim'chö ha-gödol al גְּאוּלִים לְשִׁמְךָ הַגָּדוֹל עַל

s'fas ha-yöm, yachad kulöm שְׂפַת הַיָּם, יַחַד כֻּלָּם הוֹדוּ

hodu v'himlichu v'öm'ru: וְהִמְלִיכוּ וְאָמְרוּ: יְיָ

Adonöy yim-loch l'olöm vö-ed. יִמְלֹךְ לְעוֹלָם וָעֶד.

V'ne-emar, go-alaynu adonöy וְנֶאֱמַר: גֹּאֲלֵנוּ יְיָ

108

צְבָאוֹת שְׁמוֹ קָדוֹשׁ tz'vö-os sh'mo k'dosh

יִשְׂרָאֵל. בָּרוּךְ אַתָּה יְיָ, yisrö-ayl. Böruch atöh adonöy,

גָּאַל יִשְׂרָאֵל: gö-al yisrö-ayl.

We bless God for saving us from all kinds of troubles. This prayer leads directly to the Amidah.

The Amidah

For Levels:

Ⓑ Ⓒ

עֲמִידָה

Recited standing, with feet together

[On Pesach, Shavuot, and Sukkot, a special Amidah is substituted, see Siddur]

אֲדֹנָי, שְׂפָתַי תִּפְתָּח וּפִי Adonöy, s'fösai tif-töch ufi

יַגִּיד תְּהִלָּתֶךָ: yagid t'hilö-sechö.

My Lord, open my lips, and my mouth shall declare Your praise.

Take three steps back, then three steps forward, as if approaching a king. At the word *Böruch* (blessed), bend the knee; at *Atöh* (You), bow forward; and at *Adonöy* (Lord), straighten up.

בָּרוּךְ אַתָּה יְיָ אֱלֹהֵינוּ Böruch atöh adonöy elohaynu

וֵאלֹהֵי אֲבוֹתֵינוּ, אֱלֹהֵי vay-lohay avosaynu, elohay

אַבְרָהָם, אֱלֹהֵי יִצְחָק, avröhöm, elohay yitzchök,

vay-lohay ya-akov, hö-ayl	וֵאלֹהֵי יַעֲקֹב, הָאֵל
ha-gödol ha-gibor v'hanorö,	הַגָּדוֹל הַגִּבּוֹר וְהַנּוֹרָא,
ayl el-yon, gomayl chasödim	אֵל עֶלְיוֹן, גּוֹמֵל חֲסָדִים
tovim, konay ha-kol, v'zochayr	טוֹבִים, קוֹנֵה הַכֹּל, וְזוֹכֵר
chas'day övos, umayvi go-ayl	חַסְדֵי אָבוֹת, וּמֵבִיא גוֹאֵל
liv'nay v'nayhem l'ma-an	לִבְנֵי בְנֵיהֶם לְמַעַן
sh'mo b'ahavöh.	שְׁמוֹ בְּאַהֲבָה:

Between Rosh Hashana and Yom Kippur add:

Zöch'raynu l'cha-yim,	זָכְרֵנוּ לְחַיִּים,
melech chöfaytz ba-cha-yim,	מֶלֶךְ חָפֵץ בַּחַיִּים,
v'chös'vaynu b'sayfer	וְכָתְבֵנוּ בְּסֵפֶר
ha-cha-yim, l'ma-an'chö	הַחַיִּים, לְמַעַנְךָ
elohim cha-yim.	אֱלֹהִים חַיִּים:

At the word *Böruch* (blessed), bend the knee; at *Atöh* (You), bow forward; and at *Adonöy* (Lord), straighten up.

Melech ozayr umoshi-a	מֶלֶךְ עוֹזֵר וּמוֹשִׁיעַ
umögayn. Böruch atöh	וּמָגֵן: בָּרוּךְ אַתָּה
adonöy, mögayn avröhöm.	יְיָ, מָגֵן אַבְרָהָם:

110

Blessed are You, Lord our God and God of our fathers, God of Abraham, God of Isaac and God of Jacob, the great, mighty and awesome God, exalted God, who bestows bountiful kindness, who creates all things, who remembers the piety of the Patriarchs, and who, in love, brings a redeemer to their children's children, for the sake of His Name. (*Between Rosh Hashana and Yom Kippur add*: Remember us for life, King who desires life; inscribe us in the Book of Life, for Your sake, O living God.) O King, [You are] a helper, a savior and a shield. Blessed are You Lord, Shield of Abraham.

Atöh gibor l'olöm adonöy,	אַתָּה גִבּוֹר לְעוֹלָם אֲדֹנָי,
m'cha-yeh maysim atöh,	מְחַיֶּה מֵתִים אַתָּה,
rav l'hoshi-a.	רַב לְהוֹשִׁיעַ:

In summer say: Morid ha-töl.	בקיץ: מוֹרִיד הַטָּל:
In winter say: Mashiv höru-ach	בחורף: מַשִּׁיב הָרוּחַ
umorid ha-geshem.	וּמוֹרִיד הַגֶּשֶׁם:

M'chalkayl cha-yim b'chesed,	מְכַלְכֵּל חַיִּים בְּחֶסֶד,
m'cha-yeh maysim b'rachamim	מְחַיֶּה מֵתִים בְּרַחֲמִים
rabim, somaych nof'lim,	רַבִּים, סוֹמֵךְ נוֹפְלִים,
v'rofay cholim, umatir	וְרוֹפֵא חוֹלִים, וּמַתִּיר
asurim, um'ka-yaym emunöso	אֲסוּרִים, וּמְקַיֵּם אֱמוּנָתוֹ
lishaynay öför, mi chömochö	לִישֵׁנֵי עָפָר, מִי כָמוֹךָ

111

ba-al g'vuros umi do-meh löch,   בַּעַל גְּבוּרוֹת וּמִי דּוֹמֶה לָּךְ,

melech maymis um'cha-yeh   מֶלֶךְ מֵמִית וּמְחַיֶּה

umatzmi-ach y'shu-öh.   וּמַצְמִיחַ יְשׁוּעָה:

Between Rosh Hashana and Yom Kippur add:

Mi chömochö öv hörachamön   מִי כָמוֹךָ אָב הָרַחֲמָן

(during Musaf substitute: (במוסף: הָרַחֲמִים) זוֹכֵר

hörachamim)* zochayr y'tzuröv   יְצוּרָיו לְחַיִּים

l'cha-yim b'racha-mim.   בְּרַחֲמִים:

V'ne-emön atöh l'ha-chayos   וְנֶאֱמָן אַתָּה לְהַחֲיוֹת

maysim. Boruch atöh adonöy,   מֵתִים. בָּרוּךְ אַתָּה יְיָ,

m'cha-yeh ha-maysim.   מְחַיֵּה הַמֵּתִים:

You are mighty forever, my Lord; You resurrect the dead; You are powerful to save. (*In summer say:* He causes the dew to descend.) (*In winter say:* He causes the wind to blow and the rain to fall.) He sustains the living with loving-kindness, resurrects the dead with great mercy, supports the falling, heals the sick, releases the bound, and fulfills His trust to those who sleep in the dust. Who is like You, mighty One! And who can be compared to You, King, who brings death and restores life, and causes deliverance to spring forth! (*Between Rosh Hashana and Yom Kippur add:* Who is like You, merciful Father, who in compassion remembers His creatures for life.) You are trustworthy to revive the dead. Blessed are You Lord, who revives the dead.

Continue on page 114

112

Kedusha, for during the repetition of the Amidah. Recited standing, with feet together.

Transliteration	Hebrew
Nak-dishöch v'na-ari-tzöch k'no-am si-ach	נַקְדִּישָׁךְ וְנַעֲרִיצָךְ כְּנֹעַם שִׂיחַ
sod sar'fay kodesh, ha-m'shal'shim l'chö	סוֹד שַׂרְפֵי קֹדֶשׁ, הַמְשַׁלְּשִׁים לְךָ
k'dushöh, ka-kösuv al yad n'vi-echö	קְדֻשָּׁה, כַּכָּתוּב עַל יַד נְבִיאֶךָ
v'körö zeh el zeh v'ömar.	וְקָרָא זֶה אֶל זֶה וְאָמַר :
Ködosh, ködosh, ködosh, adonöy	קָדוֹשׁ, קָדוֹשׁ, קָדוֹשׁ יְיָ
tz'vö-os, m'lo chöl hö-öretz k'vodo.	צְבָאוֹת, מְלֹא כָל הָאָרֶץ כְּבוֹדוֹ :
Öz b'kol ra-ash gödol adir v'chözök,	אָז, בְּקוֹל רַעַשׁ גָּדוֹל אַדִּיר וְחָזָק,
mashmi-im kol, misna-s'im	מַשְׁמִיעִים קוֹל, מִתְנַשְּׂאִים
l'umas has'röfim, l'umösöm	לְעֻמַּת הַשְּׂרָפִים, לְעֻמָּתָם
m'shab'chim v'om'rim.	מְשַׁבְּחִים וְאוֹמְרִים :
Böruch k'vod adonöy mim'kómo.	בָּרוּךְ כְּבוֹד יְיָ מִמְּקוֹמוֹ :
Mim'komöch malkaynu sofi-a v'simloch	מִמְּקוֹמְךָ מַלְכֵּנוּ תוֹפִיעַ וְתִמְלוֹךְ
ölaynu ki m'chakim anach-nu löch mösai	עָלֵינוּ, כִּי מְחַכִּים אֲנַחְנוּ לָךְ מָתַי
tim-loch b'tziyon, b'körov b'yömaynu	תִּמְלֹךְ בְּצִיּוֹן, בְּקָרוֹב בְּיָמֵינוּ
l'olöm vö-ed. Tishkon tis-gadayl	לְעוֹלָם וָעֶד. תִּשְׁכּוֹן תִּתְגַּדֵּל
v'siska-daysh b'soch y'rushöla-yim ir'chö,	וְתִתְקַדֵּשׁ בְּתוֹךְ יְרוּשָׁלַיִם עִירְךָ,
l'dor vödor ul'naytzach n'tzöchim.	לְדוֹר וָדוֹר וּלְנֵצַח נְצָחִים :
V'ay-naynu sir-enöh mal'chu-sechö,	וְעֵינֵינוּ תִרְאֶינָה מַלְכוּתֶךָ,
ka-dövör hö-ömur b'shiray uzechö,	כַּדָּבָר הָאָמוּר בְּשִׁירֵי עֻזֶּךָ,
al y'day dövid m'shi-ach tzidkechö.	עַל יְדֵי דָוִד מְשִׁיחַ צִדְקֶךָ :
Yimloch adonöy l'olöm eloha-yich	יִמְלֹךְ יְיָ לְעוֹלָם אֱלֹהַיִךְ
tziyon l'dor vö-dor ha-l'luyöh.	צִיּוֹן לְדֹר וָדֹר, הַלְלוּיָהּ :

Atöh ködosh v'shim'chö אַתָּה קָדוֹשׁ וְשִׁמְךָ

ködosh uk'doshim b'chöl yom קָדוֹשׁ וּקְדוֹשִׁים בְּכָל יוֹם

y'ha-l'luchö selöh. Boruch atöh יְהַלְלוּךָ סֶּלָה. בָּרוּךְ אַתָּה

adonöy, hö-ayl ha-ködosh. יְיָ, הָאֵל הַקָּדוֹשׁ:

(Between Rosh Hashana and Yom (בשבת שובה:

Kippur subsitute: Ha-melech ha-ködosh.) הַמֶּלֶךְ הַקָּדוֹשׁ)

You are holy and Your Name is holy, and holy beings praise You daily for all eternity. Blessed are You Lord, the holy God. *(Between Rosh Hashana and Yom Kippur substitute:* the holy King.)

Level 6 continues below:

Yismach mosheh b'mat'nas יִשְׂמַח מֹשֶׁה בְּמַתְּנַת

chel-ko, ki eved ne-emön חֶלְקוֹ, כִּי עֶבֶד נֶאֱמָן

körösö lo, k'lil tif-eres קָרָאתָ לּוֹ, כְּלִיל תִּפְאֶרֶת

b'rosho nösatö lo b'öm'do בְּרֹאשׁוֹ נָתַתָּ לּוֹ בְּעָמְדוֹ

l'fö-nechö al har sinai לְפָנֶיךָ עַל הַר סִינַי,

ush'nay luchos avönim וּשְׁנֵי לוּחוֹת אֲבָנִים

ho-rid b'yödo, v'chösuv הוֹרִיד בְּיָדוֹ, וְכָתוּב

114

bö-hem sh'miras shabös, בָּהֶם שְׁמִירַת שַׁבָּת,

v'chayn kösuv b'sorösechö. וְכֵן כָּתוּב בְּתוֹרָתֶךָ:

Moses rejoiced in the gift of his portion, for You called him a faithful servant. And he brought down two tablets of stone in his hand, on which was inscribed the observance of Shabbat; and so it is written in Your Torah:

V'shöm'ru v'nay yisrö-ayl es וְשָׁמְרוּ בְנֵי יִשְׂרָאֵל אֶת

ha-shabös, la-asos es ha-shabös הַשַּׁבָּת, לַעֲשׂוֹת אֶת הַשַּׁבָּת

l'dorosöm b'ris olöm. Bayni לְדֹרֹתָם בְּרִית עוֹלָם: בֵּינִי

uvayn b'nay yisrö-ayl os hee וּבֵין בְּנֵי יִשְׂרָאֵל אוֹת הִיא

l'olöm, ki shay-shes yömim לְעוֹלָם, כִּי שֵׁשֶׁת יָמִים

ösöh adonöy es ha-shöma-yim עָשָׂה יְיָ אֶת הַשָּׁמַיִם

v'es hö-öretz uva-yom וְאֶת הָאָרֶץ, וּבַיּוֹם

ha-sh'vi-i shövas va-yinöfash. הַשְּׁבִיעִי שָׁבַת וַיִּנָּפַשׁ:

And the children of Israel shall observe the Shabbat, establishing the Shabbat throughout their generations as an everlasting covenant. It is a sign between Me and the children of Israel for all time, for in six days the Lord made the heavens and the earth, and on the seventh day He ceased from work and rested.

V'lo n'sato adonöy elohaynu וְלֹא נְתַתּוֹ יְיָ אֱלֹהֵינוּ

l'go-yay hö-arötzos, v'lo לְגוֹיֵי הָאֲרָצוֹת, וְלֹא

hin-chalto malkaynu l'ov'day הִנְחַלְתּוֹ מַלְכֵּנוּ לְעוֹבְדֵי

115

elilim, v'gam bim'nuchöso lo אֱלִילִים, וְגַם בִּמְנוּחָתוֹ לֹא

yish-k'nu araylim, ki l'yisrö-ayl יִשְׁכְּנוּ עֲרֵלִים, כִּי לְיִשְׂרָאֵל

am'chö n'sato b'a-havöh, עַמְּךָ נְתַתּוֹ בְּאַהֲבָה,

l'zera ya-akov, asher לְזֶרַע יַעֲקֹב, אֲשֶׁר

böm böchör-tö. בָּם בָּחָרְתָּ.

And You, Lord our God, did not give it [the Shabbat] to the nations of the world, nor did You, our King, grant it as a heritage to idol-worshippers, nor can the uncircumcised participate in its rest — for You have given it in love to Your people Israel, to the descendants of Jacob whom You have chosen.

Yis-m'chu v'mal'chus'chö יִשְׂמְחוּ בְמַלְכוּתְךָ

shom'ray shabös v'kor'ay oneg, שׁוֹמְרֵי שַׁבָּת וְקוֹרְאֵי עֹנֶג,

am m'kad'shay sh'vi-i, kulöm עַם מְקַדְּשֵׁי שְׁבִיעִי, כֻּלָּם

yis-b'u v'yis-an'gu mituvechö, יִשְׂבְּעוּ וְיִתְעַנְּגוּ מִטּוּבֶךָ,

uvash'vi-i rö-tzisö bo וּבַשְּׁבִיעִי רָצִיתָ בּוֹ

v'kidashto, chemdas yömim וְקִדַּשְׁתּוֹ, חֶמְדַּת יָמִים

oso körösö. (*During Musaf add:* אוֹתוֹ קָרָאתָ. (במוסף: זֵכֶר

Zaycher l'ma-asay v'rayshis.) לְמַעֲשֵׂה בְרֵאשִׁית:)

Those who observe the Shabbat and call it a delight shall rejoice in Your kingship; the nation which hallows the Seventh Day — all shall be satiated and delighted with Your goodness. You were pleased with the Seventh Day and made it holy; You called it the most desirable of days. (*During Musaf add:* In remembrance of the work of Creation.)

Elohaynu vay-lohay avosay-nu,	אֱלֹהֵינוּ וֵאלֹהֵי אֲבוֹתֵינוּ,
r'tzay nö vim'nuchösaynu,	רְצֵה נָא בִמְנוּחָתֵנוּ,
kad'shaynu b'mitzvosechö	קַדְּשֵׁנוּ בְּמִצְוֹתֶיךָ
v'sayn chel-kaynu b'sorösechö,	וְתֵן חֶלְקֵנוּ בְּתוֹרָתֶךָ,
sab'aynu mi-tuvechö	שַׂבְּעֵנוּ מִטּוּבֶךָ
v'samay-ach naf-shaynu	וְשַׂמֵּחַ נַפְשֵׁנוּ
bishu-ösechö, v'tahayr libaynu	בִּישׁוּעָתֶךָ, וְטַהֵר לִבֵּנוּ
l'öv-d'chö be-emes,	לְעָבְדְּךָ בֶּאֱמֶת,
v'han-chi-laynu adonöy	וְהַנְחִילֵנוּ יְיָ
elohaynu b'ahavöh	אֱלֹהֵינוּ בְּאַהֲבָה
uv'rö-tzon shabas köd-shechö,	וּבְרָצוֹן שַׁבַּת קָדְשֶׁךָ,
v'yönuchu vö köl yisrö-ayl	וְיָנוּחוּ בוֹ כָּל יִשְׂרָאֵל
m'kad'shay sh'mechö.	מְקַדְּשֵׁי שְׁמֶךָ:
Boruch atöh adonöy,	בָּרוּךְ אַתָּה יְיָ,
m'kadaysh ha-shabös.	מְקַדֵּשׁ הַשַּׁבָּת:

Our God and God of our fathers, please find favor in our rest, make us holy with Your commandments and grant us our portion in Your Torah; satiate us with Your goodness, gladden our soul with Your salvation, and make our heart pure to serve You in truth; and, Lord our God, grant as our heritage, in love and goodwill, Your holy Shabbat, and may all Israel who sanctify Your Name rest thereon. Blessed are You Lord, who sanctifies Shabbat.

R'tzay, adonöy elohaynu,	רְצֵה, יְיָ אֱלֹהֵינוּ,
b'am'chö yisrö-ayl, v'lis'filösöm	בְּעַמְּךָ יִשְׂרָאֵל, וְלִתְפִלָּתָם
sh'ay, v'höshayv hö-avodöh	שְׁעֵה, וְהָשֵׁב הָעֲבוֹדָה
lid'vir bay-sechö, v'ishay	לִדְבִיר בֵּיתֶךָ, וְאִשֵּׁי
yisrö-ayl us'filösöm b'ahavöh	יִשְׂרָאֵל וּתְפִלָּתָם בְּאַהֲבָה
s'kabayl b'rö-tzon, us'hi	תְקַבֵּל בְּרָצוֹן, וּתְהִי
l'rö-tzon tömid avodas	לְרָצוֹן תָּמִיד עֲבוֹדַת
yisrö-ayl amechö.	יִשְׂרָאֵל עַמֶּךָ:

Look with favor, Lord our God, on Your people Israel and pay heed to their prayer; restore the service to Your Sanctuary and accept with love and favor Israel's fire-offerings and prayer; and may the service of Your people Israel always find favor.

On Rosh Chodesh and Festivals, add the following during the Morning service. During Musaf, refer to a regular Siddur for special additions:

Elohaynu vay-lohay avosaynu	אֱלֹהֵינוּ וֵאלֹהֵי אֲבוֹתֵינוּ
ya-aleh v'yövo, v'yagi-a v'yayrö-eh	יַעֲלֶה וְיָבֹא, וְיַגִּיעַ וְיֵרָאֶה
v'yay-rötzeh, v'yishöma v'yipökayd	וְיֵרָצֶה, וְיִשָּׁמַע וְיִפָּקֵד
v'yizöchayr, zichro-naynu	וְיִזָּכֵר, זִכְרוֹנֵנוּ
ufik'do-naynu, v'zichron	וּפִקְדוֹנֵנוּ, וְזִכְרוֹן
avosaynu, v'zichron möshi-ach	אֲבוֹתֵינוּ, וְזִכְרוֹן מָשִׁיחַ
ben dövid avdechö, v'zichron	בֶּן דָּוִד עַבְדֶּךָ, וְזִכְרוֹן
y'rushöla-yim ir köd-shechö,	יְרוּשָׁלַיִם עִיר קָדְשֶׁךָ,
v'zichron köl am'chö bays yisrö-ayl	וְזִכְרוֹן כָּל עַמְּךָ בֵּית יִשְׂרָאֵל
l'fönechö lif'laytöh l'tovöh, l'chayn	לְפָנֶיךָ לִפְלֵיטָה לְטוֹבָה, לְחֵן

118

ul'chesed ul'rachamim ul'cha-yim	וּלְחֶסֶד וּלְרַחֲמִים וּלְחַיִּים
tovim ul'shölom b'yom	טוֹבִים וּלְשָׁלוֹם, בְּיוֹם

On Rosh Chodesh:	בר״ח:
Rosh ha-chodesh ha-zeh.	רֹאשׁ הַחֹדֶשׁ הַזֶּה.
On Pesach:	בפסח:
Chag ha-matzos ha-zeh.	חַג הַמַּצּוֹת הַזֶּה.
On Sukkot:	בסוכות:
Chag ha-sukos ha-zeh.	חַג הַסֻּכּוֹת הַזֶּה.

Zöch'raynu adonöy elohaynu bo	זָכְרֵנוּ יְיָ אֱלֹהֵינוּ בּוֹ
l'tovöh, ufök'daynu vo liv'röchöh	לְטוֹבָה, וּפָקְדֵנוּ בוֹ לִבְרָכָה,
v'hoshi-aynu vo l'cha-yim tovim.	וְהוֹשִׁיעֵנוּ בוֹ לְחַיִּים טוֹבִים:
Uvid'var y'shu-öh v'rachamim	וּבִדְבַר יְשׁוּעָה וְרַחֲמִים
chus v'chönaynu v'rachaym ölaynu	חוּס וְחָנֵּנוּ וְרַחֵם עָלֵינוּ
v'hoshi-aynu ki aylechö aynaynu,	וְהוֹשִׁיעֵנוּ כִּי אֵלֶיךָ עֵינֵינוּ,
ki ayl melech chanun	כִּי אֵל מֶלֶךְ חַנּוּן
v'rachum ötöh.	וְרַחוּם אָתָּה:

Our God and God of our fathers, may there ascend, come and reach, be seen, accepted, and heard, recalled and remembered before You, the remembrance and recollection of us, the remembrance of our fathers, the remembrance of *Moshiach* the son of David Your servant, the remembrance of Jerusalem Your holy city, and the remembrance of all Your people the House of Israel, for deliverance, well-being, grace, kindness, mercy, good life and peace, on this day of: *On Rosh Chodesh:* Rosh Chodesh. *On Pesach:* the Festival of Matzot. *On Sukkot:* the Festival of Sukkot. Remember us on this [day], Lord our God, for good; be mindful of us on this [day] for blessing; help us on this [day] for good life. With the promise of deliverance and compassion, spare us and be gracious to us; have mercy upon us and deliver us; for our eyes are directed to You, for You, God, are a gracious and merciful King.

V'se-chezenöh aynaynu	וְתֶחֱזֶינָה עֵינֵינוּ
b'shuv'chö l'tziyon	בְּשׁוּבְךָ לְצִיּוֹן
b'rachamim. Böruch atöh	בְּרַחֲמִים. בָּרוּךְ אַתָּה
adonöy, ha-machazir	יְיָ, הַמַּחֲזִיר
sh'chinöso l'tziyon.	שְׁכִינָתוֹ לְצִיּוֹן׃

May our eyes behold Your return to Zion in mercy. Blessed are You Lord, who restores His Divine Presence to Zion.

Level 𝔅 resumes here.
Bow forward when saying the first five words of *Modim*.

Modim anachnu löch,	מוֹדִים אֲנַחְנוּ לָךְ,
shö-atöh hu adonöy elohaynu	שָׁאַתָּה הוּא יְיָ אֱלֹהֵינוּ
vay-lohay avosaynu l'olöm	וֵאלֹהֵי אֲבוֹתֵינוּ לְעוֹלָם
vö-ed, tzur cha-yaynu mögayn	וָעֶד, צוּר חַיֵּינוּ מָגֵן
yish-aynu, atöh hu l'dor	יִשְׁעֵנוּ, אַתָּה הוּא לְדוֹר
vödor, no-deh l'chö un'sapayr	וָדוֹר, נוֹדֶה לְּךָ וּנְסַפֵּר
t'hilösechö, al cha-yaynu	תְּהִלָּתֶךָ, עַל חַיֵּינוּ
ha-m'surim b'yödechö,	הַמְּסוּרִים בְּיָדֶךָ,
v'al nish'mosaynu ha-p'kudos	וְעַל נִשְׁמוֹתֵינוּ הַפְּקוּדוֹת

120

löch, v'al nisechö sheb'chöl	לָךְ, וְעַל נִסֶּיךָ שֶׁבְּכָל
yom imönu, v'al nif-l'ösechö	יוֹם עִמָּנוּ, וְעַל נִפְלְאוֹתֶיךָ
v'tovosechö sheb'chöl ays erev	וְטוֹבוֹתֶיךָ שֶׁבְּכָל עֵת, עֶרֶב
vövoker v'tzöhörö-yim, ha-tov,	וָבֹקֶר וְצָהֳרָיִם, הַטּוֹב,
ki lo chölu ra-chamechö,	כִּי לֹא כָלוּ רַחֲמֶיךָ,
v'ham'rachaym, ki lo samu	וְהַמְרַחֵם, כִּי לֹא תַמּוּ
chasö-dechö, ki may-olöm	חֲסָדֶיךָ, כִּי מֵעוֹלָם
kivinu löch.	קִוִּינוּ לָךְ:

We thankfully acknowledge that You are the Lord our God and God of our fathers forever. You are the strength of our life, the shield of our salvation in every generation. We will give thanks to You and recount Your praise, evening, morning and noon, for our lives which are committed into Your hand, for our souls which are entrusted to You, for Your miracles which are with us daily, and for Your continual wonders and beneficences. You are the Beneficent One, for Your mercies never cease; and the Merciful One, for Your kindnesses never end; for we always place our hope in You.

Modim, for during the repetition of the Amidah. Recited standing. Bow your head while reciting the first five words of Modim.

Modim anach-nu löch, shö-atöh hu	מוֹדִים אֲנַחְנוּ לָךְ, שָׁאַתָּה הוּא
adonöy elo-haynu vay-lohay avosaynu,	יְיָ אֱלֹהֵינוּ וֵאלֹהֵי אֲבוֹתֵינוּ,
elohay köl bösör, yo-tz'raynu, yo-tzayr	אֱלֹהֵי כָּל בָּשָׂר, יוֹצְרֵנוּ, יוֹצֵר
b'rayshis. B'röchos v'hodö-os l'shim'chö	בְּרֵאשִׁית, בְּרָכוֹת וְהוֹדָאוֹת לְשִׁמְךָ
ha-gödol v'haködosh, al she-heche-yisönu	הַגָּדוֹל וְהַקָּדוֹשׁ, עַל שֶׁהֶחֱיִיתָנוּ

121

v'kiyam-tönu. kayn t'cha-yaynu	וְקַיְמָתָּנוּ. כֵּן תְּחַיֵּינוּ
us'ka-y'maynu v'se-esof gölu-yosay-nu	וּתְקַיְּמֵנוּ, וְתֶאֱסוֹף גָּלֻיּוֹתֵינוּ
l'chatz'ros köd-shechö, v'nö-suv ay-lechö	לְחַצְרוֹת קָדְשֶׁךָ, וְנָשׁוּב אֵלֶיךָ
lishmor chukechö, v'la-asos r'tzonechö,	לִשְׁמוֹר חֻקֶּיךָ, וְלַעֲשׂוֹת רְצוֹנֶךָ,
ul'öv-d'chö b'layvöv shölaym, al she-önu	וּלְעָבְדְּךָ בְּלֵבָב שָׁלֵם, עַל שֶׁאָנוּ
modim löch. Böruch ayl ha-hodö-os.	מוֹדִים לָךְ, בָּרוּךְ אֵל הַהוֹדָאוֹת:

During Chanukah add "V'al Hanisim" (see regular Siddur).
Otherwise continue below.

V'al kulöm yis-böraych	וְעַל כֻּלָּם יִתְבָּרֵךְ
v'yisromöm v'yisnasay	וְיִתְרוֹמָם וְיִתְנַשֵּׂא
shim'chö malkaynu	שִׁמְךָ מַלְכֵּנוּ
tömid l'olöm vö-ed.	תָּמִיד לְעוֹלָם וָעֶד:

And for all these, may Your Name, our King, be continually blessed, exalted and extolled forever and all time.

Between Rosh Hashana and Yom Kippur add:

Uch'sov l'cha-yim tovim	וּכְתוֹב לְחַיִּים טוֹבִים
köl b'nay v'risechö.	כָּל בְּנֵי בְרִיתֶךָ:

Inscribe all the children of Your Covenant for a good life.

At the word *Böruch* (blessed), bend the knee; at *Atöh* (You), bow forward; and at *Adonöy* (Lord), straighten up.

V'chöl ha-cha-yim yo-duchö	וְכָל הַחַיִּים יוֹדוּךָ
selöh vihal'lu shim'chö	סֶּלָה וִיהַלְלוּ שִׁמְךָ
ha-gödol l'olöm ki tov,	הַגָּדוֹל לְעוֹלָם כִּי טוֹב,
hö-ayl y'shu-ösaynu	הָאֵל יְשׁוּעָתֵנוּ
v'ezrösaynu selöh, hö-ayl	וְעֶזְרָתֵנוּ סֶלָה, הָאֵל
ha-tov. Boruch atöh adonöy,	הַטּוֹב. בָּרוּךְ אַתָּה יְיָ,
ha-tov shim'chö ul'chö	הַטּוֹב שִׁמְךָ וּלְךָ
nö-eh l'hodos.	נָאֶה לְהוֹדוֹת:

And all living things shall forever thank You, and praise Your great Name eternally, for You are good. God, You are our everlasting salvation and help, O benevolent God. Blessed are You Lord, Beneficent is Your Name, and to You it is fitting to offer thanks.

Sim shölom tovöh uv'röchöh,	שִׂים שָׁלוֹם, טוֹבָה וּבְרָכָה,
cha-yim chayn vöchesed	חַיִּים חֵן וָחֶסֶד
v'rachamim, ölaynu v'al köl	וְרַחֲמִים, עָלֵינוּ וְעַל כָּל
yisrö-ayl amechö. Bö-r'chaynu	יִשְׂרָאֵל עַמֶּךָ. בָּרְכֵנוּ
övinu kulönu k'echöd	אָבִינוּ כֻּלָּנוּ כְּאֶחָד,
b'or pönechö, ki v'or	בְּאוֹר פָּנֶיךָ, כִּי בְאוֹר
pönechö, nösatö lönu, adonöy	פָּנֶיךָ, נָתַתָּ לָנוּ יְיָ

elohaynu, toras cha-yim	אֱלֹהֵינוּ תּוֹרַת חַיִּים,
v'ahavas chesed utz'dököh	וְאַהֲבַת חֶסֶד, וּצְדָקָה
uv'röchöh v'rachamim	וּבְרָכָה וְרַחֲמִים
v'cha-yim v'shölom.	וְחַיִּים וְשָׁלוֹם.
V'tov b'aynechö l'vöraych es	וְטוֹב בְּעֵינֶיךָ לְבָרֵךְ אֶת
am'chö yisrö-ayl b'chöl ays	עַמְּךָ יִשְׂרָאֵל בְּכָל עֵת
uv'chöl shö-öh bish'lomechö.	וּבְכָל שָׁעָה בִּשְׁלוֹמֶךָ.

Bestow peace, goodness and blessing, life, graciousness, kindness and mercy, upon us and upon all Your people Israel. Bless us, our Father, all of us as one, with the light of Your countenance. For by the light of Your countenance You gave us, Lord our God, the Torah of life and loving-kindness, righteousness, blessing, mercy, life and peace. May it be favorable in Your eyes to bless Your people Israel, at all times and at every moment, with Your peace.

Between Rosh Hashana and Yom Kippur add:

Uv'sayfer cha-yim b'röchöh	וּבְסֵפֶר חַיִּים בְּרָכָה
v'shölom ufarnösöh tovöh,	וְשָׁלוֹם וּפַרְנָסָה טוֹבָה
y'shu-öh v'nechömöh, ug'zayros	יְשׁוּעָה וְנֶחָמָה וּגְזֵרוֹת
tovos, nizöchayr v'nikösayv	טוֹבוֹת נִזָּכֵר וְנִכָּתֵב
l'fönechö, anachnu v'chöl am'chö	לְפָנֶיךָ, אֲנַחְנוּ וְכָל עַמְּךָ
bays yisrö-ayl, l'cha-yim	בֵּית יִשְׂרָאֵל, לְחַיִּים
tovim ul'shölom.	טוֹבִים וּלְשָׁלוֹם.

And in the Book of Life, blessing, peace and prosperity, deliverance, consolation and

124

favorable decrees, may we and all Your people the House of Israel be remembered and inscribed before You for a happy life and for peace.

Boruch atöh adonöy,   בָּרוּךְ אַתָּה יְיָ,

ha-m'võraych es amo   הַמְבָרֵךְ אֶת עַמּוֹ

yisrö-ayl ba-shölom.   יִשְׂרָאֵל בַּשָּׁלוֹם:

Blessed are You Lord, who blesses His people Israel with peace.

Yih-yu l'rö-tzon im'ray fi,   יִהְיוּ לְרָצוֹן אִמְרֵי פִי,

v'heg-yon libi l'fönechö,   וְהֶגְיוֹן לִבִּי לְפָנֶיךָ,

adonöy tzuri v'go-ali.   יְיָ צוּרִי וְגוֹאֲלִי.

May the words of my mouth and the meditation of my heart be acceptable before You, Lord, my Strength and my Redeemer.

Elohai, n'tzor l'shoni may-rö,   אֱלֹהַי, נְצוֹר לְשׁוֹנִי מֵרָע,

us'fösai midabayr mirmöh.   וּשְׂפָתַי מִדַּבֵּר מִרְמָה.

V'lim'kal'lai, nafshi sidom,   וְלִמְקַלְלַי, נַפְשִׁי תִדּוֹם,

v'nafshi ke-öför la-kol tih-yeh.   וְנַפְשִׁי כֶּעָפָר לַכֹּל תִּהְיֶה.

P'sach libi b'sorösechö,   פְּתַח לִבִּי בְּתוֹרָתֶךָ,

uv'mitzvosechö tirdof nafshi,   וּבְמִצְוֹתֶיךָ תִּרְדּוֹף נַפְשִׁי,

v'chöl ha-chosh'vim ölai rö-öh,   וְכָל הַחוֹשְׁבִים עָלַי רָעָה,

m'hayröh höfayr atzösöm	מְהֵרָה הָפֵר עֲצָתָם
v'kalkayl ma-chashavtöm.	וְקַלְקֵל מַחֲשַׁבְתָּם.
Yih-yu k'motz lif'nay ru-ach	יִהְיוּ כְּמוֹץ לִפְנֵי רוּחַ
umal-ach adonöy do-cheh.	וּמַלְאַךְ יְיָ דּוֹחֶה.
L'ma-an yay-chöl'tzun	לְמַעַן יֵחָלְצוּן
y'didechö, hoshi-öh y'min'chö	יְדִידֶיךָ, הוֹשִׁיעָה יְמִינְךָ
va-anayni. Asay l'ma-an	וַעֲנֵנִי. עֲשֵׂה לְמַעַן
sh'mechö, asay l'ma-an	שְׁמֶךָ, עֲשֵׂה לְמַעַן
y'minechö, asay l'ma-an	יְמִינֶךָ, עֲשֵׂה לְמַעַן
torösechö, asay l'ma-an	תּוֹרָתֶךָ, עֲשֵׂה לְמַעַן
k'dusho-sechö. Yih-yu	קְדֻשָּׁתֶךָ. יִהְיוּ
l'rö-tzon im'ray fi, v'heg-yon	לְרָצוֹן אִמְרֵי פִי, וְהֶגְיוֹן
libi l'fönechö, adonöy	לִבִּי לְפָנֶיךָ, יְיָ
tzuri v'go-ali.	צוּרִי וְגוֹאֲלִי.

My God, guard my tongue from evil and my lips from speaking deceitfully. Let my soul be silent to those who curse me; let my soul be as dust to all. Open my heart to Your Torah, and let my soul eagerly pursue Your commandments. As for all those who plot evil against me, hasten to annul their counsel and frustrate their design. Let them be as chaff before the wind; let the angel of the Lord thrust them away. That Your beloved ones may be delivered, help with Your right hand and answer me. Do it for the sake of Your Name; do it for the sake of Your right hand; do it for the sake of Your Torah; do it for the sake of

Your holiness. May the words of my mouth and the meditation of my heart be acceptable before You, Lord, my Strength and my Redeemer.

Take three steps back and say:

עֹשֶׂה שָׁלוֹם (בש״ת: הַשָּׁלוֹם) O-seh shölom (*Between Rosh Hashana*

and Yom Kippur: ha-shölom) bim'romöv, בִּמְרוֹמָיו, הוּא יַעֲשֶׂה שָׁלוֹם

hu ya-aseh shölom ölaynu v'al עָלֵינוּ וְעַל כָּל יִשְׂרָאֵל,

köl yisrö-ayl, v'im'ru ömayn. וְאִמְרוּ אָמֵן:

He who makes peace (*Between Rosh Hashana and Yom Kippur substitute:* the peace) in His heavens, may He make peace for us and for all Israel; and say: Amen.

Y'hi rö-tzon mil'fönechö, יְהִי רָצוֹן מִלְּפָנֶיךָ,

adonöy elohaynu vay-lohay יְיָ אֱלֹהֵינוּ וֵאלֹהֵי

avosaynu, she-yibö-neh bays אֲבוֹתֵינוּ, שֶׁיִּבָּנֶה בֵּית

ha-mikdösh bim'hayröh הַמִּקְדָּשׁ בִּמְהֵרָה

v'yömaynu, v'sayn בְיָמֵינוּ, וְתֵן

chelkaynu b'sörösechö. חֶלְקֵנוּ בְּתוֹרָתֶךָ.

May it be Your will, Lord our God and God of our fathers, that the *Beit Hamikdash* (Holy Temple) be speedily rebuilt in our days, and grant us our portion in Your Torah.

Take three steps forward.

On Rosh Chodesh and Festivals "Hallel" is recited here (see regular Siddur).

Reading the Torah **For Levels:** קְרִיאַת הַתּוֹרָה
ⓑ ⓒ

Since the time that God gave the Torah to the Jewish people on mount Sinai, over 3,300 years ago, Moses assembled all the people and read them sections from the Torah pertaining to Shabbat and the Festivals. The Torah readings are generally as follows: On Shabbat the weekly portion is read, and seven male Jewish adults are "called up" to have a portion of the Sidra read to each. An eighth person is called up for Maftir and Haftarah (a chapter from the Prophets).

The reading of the Torah is most important, for the Torah is the holiest thing we, as Jews, possess; it is the wisdom of God, and contains the commandments God desires us to observe and fulfill in our everyday life.

Every time we take the Torah from the Ark, we are reminded of that great event when the Torah was first given to us by God on Mount Sinai. All the people stood and trembled in the presence of God. It may be too much to expect of us to feel exactly the same way every time we see the Torah taken from the Ark, but at least something of those exciting feelings that our ancestors felt on that occasion should enter our heart and mind when the same Torah is taken out to be read to us.

Before the Torah is taken out of the Ark, we recite the following:

Va-y'hi bin'so-a hö-öron	וַיְהִי בִּנְסֹעַ הָאָרֹן
va-yomer mosheh: Kumöh	וַיֹּאמֶר מֹשֶׁה: קוּמָה
adonöy, v'yöfu-tzu o-y'vechö,	יְיָ וְיָפֻצוּ אֹיְבֶיךָ
v'yönusu m'san'echö	וְיָנֻסוּ מְשַׂנְאֶיךָ
mi-pönechö. Ki mi-tzi-yon	מִפָּנֶיךָ: כִּי מִצִּיּוֹן
tay-tzay soröh, ud'var adonöy	תֵּצֵא תוֹרָה וּדְבַר יְיָ
miru-shölö-yim. Böruch	מִירוּשָׁלָיִם: בָּרוּךְ
shenösan toröh l'amo	שֶׁנָּתַן תּוֹרָה לְעַמּוֹ
yisrö-ayl bik'dushöso.	יִשְׂרָאֵל בִּקְדֻשָּׁתוֹ:

We bless God for having given us the Torah "with His holiness." A holy way of life is one in which everything we do is dedicated to God.

At the conclusion of the reading of the Torah, as the Torah is lifted, we say the following:

V'zos ha-toröh asher söm	וְזֹאת הַתּוֹרָה אֲשֶׁר שָׂם
mosheh lif'nay b'nay yisrö-ayl.	מֹשֶׁה לִפְנֵי בְּנֵי יִשְׂרָאֵל:
Aytz cha-yim hi lama-chazikim	עֵץ חַיִּים הִיא לַמַּחֲזִיקִים
böh, v'som'chehö m'ushör.	בָּהּ, וְתֹמְכֶיהָ מְאֻשָּׁר:

D'röchehö dar'chay no-am,	דְּרָכֶיהָ דַרְכֵי נֹעַם,
v'chöl n'sivo-sehö shölom.	וְכָל נְתִיבוֹתֶיהָ שָׁלוֹם :
Orech yömim bi-minöh,	אֹרֶךְ יָמִים בִּימִינָהּ,
bis'molöh osher v'chövod.	בִּשְׂמֹאלָהּ עֹשֶׁר וְכָבוֹד :
Adonöy chöfaytz l'ma-an tzidko	יְיָ חָפֵץ לְמַעַן צִדְקוֹ,
yagdil toröh v'ya-dir.	יַגְדִיל תּוֹרָה וְיַאְדִּיר :

Here we are proudly stating that this is the same Torah which Moses placed before the children of Israel over 3,300 years ago. Nothing in it has changed. And it is as relevant today as it was then.

The Blessing For the New Month

For Levels: Ⓖ

בִּרְכַּת הַחוֹדֶשׁ

On the Shabbat before the beginning of a new month, the following blessing is recited before the Torah is returned to the ark.

Mi she-ösö nisim la-avosaynu,	מִי שֶׁעָשָׂה נִסִּים לַאֲבוֹתֵינוּ,
v'gö-al osöm may-av'dus l'chay-rus,	וְגָאַל אוֹתָם מֵעַבְדוּת לְחֵרוּת,
hu yig-al osönu b'körov, vi-kabaytz	הוּא יִגְאַל אוֹתָנוּ בְּקָרוֹב, וִיקַבֵּץ
ni-döchaynu may-arba kan'fos	נִדָּחֵינוּ מֵאַרְבַּע כַּנְפוֹת
hö-öretz, cha-vayrim köl yisrö-ayl,	הָאָרֶץ, חֲבֵרִים כָּל יִשְׂרָאֵל,
v'nomar ömayn.	וְנֹאמַר אָמֵן :

130

Rosh chodesh (month) ba-yom (day of the week) ha-böh ölaynu l'tovöh.	רֹאשׁ חֹדֶשׁ (פלוני) בַּיוֹם (פלוני) הַבָּא עָלֵינוּ לְטוֹבָה :
Y'chad'shay-hu ha-ködosh böruch hu ölaynu, v'al köl amo bays yisrö-ayl, l'cha-yim ul'shölom, l'sösön ul'simchöh, lishu-öh ul'ne-chömöh, v'nomar ömayn.	יְחַדְּשֵׁהוּ הַקָּדוֹשׁ בָּרוּךְ הוּא עָלֵינוּ, וְעַל כָּל עַמּוֹ בֵּית יִשְׂרָאֵל, לְחַיִּים וּלְשָׁלוֹם, לְשָׂשׂוֹן וּלְשִׂמְחָה, לִישׁוּעָה וּלְנֶחָמָה, וְנֹאמַר אָמֵן :

May He who performed miracles for our fathers and redeemed them from slavery to freedom, speedily redeem us and gather our dispersed people from the four corners of the earth, uniting all Israel; and let us say, Amen. Rosh Chodesh (*Name of the month*) will be on (*Name the day or days of the week on which it falls*) which comes to us for good. May the Holy One, blessed be He, renew it for us and for all His people, the House of Israel, for life and for peace, for gladness and for joy, for deliverance and for consolation; and let us say, Amen.

Musaf — מוּסָף

For Levels:
B C

For the Musaf Amidah prayer, turn to page 109 and say through הָאֵל הַקָּדוֹשׁ (hö-ayl haködosh), page 114, then add the two portions below.

Tikan-tö shabös rö-tzisö	תִּקַּנְתָּ שַׁבָּת רָצִיתָ
kör-b'nosehö, tzivisö	קָרְבְּנוֹתֶיהָ, צִוִּיתָ
payrushe-hö im si-duray	פֵּרוּשֶׁיהָ עִם סִדּוּרֵי

131

n'söchehö. M'an'gehö l'olöm	נִסְכֶּיהָ: מְעַנְּגֶיהָ לְעוֹלָם
kövod yin-chölu, to-amehö	כָּבוֹד יִנְחָלוּ, טוֹעֲמֶיהָ
cha-yim zöchu, v'gam	חַיִּים זָכוּ, וְגַם
hö-ohavim d'vörehö g'dulöh	הָאוֹהֲבִים דְּבָרֶיהָ גְּדֻלָּה
böchöru, öz mi-sinai nitz-tavu	בָּחָרוּ, אָז מִסִּינַי נִצְטַוּוּ
tzivu-yay pö-ölehö körö-uy.	צִוּוּיֵי פְּעֻלֶיהָ כָּרָאוּי:
Y'hi rö-tzon mil'fönechö,	יְהִי רָצוֹן מִלְּפָנֶיךָ,
adonöy elohaynu vay-lohay	יְיָ אֱלֹהֵינוּ וֵאלֹהֵי
avosaynu, she-ta-alaynu	אֲבוֹתֵינוּ, שֶׁתַּעֲלֵנוּ
v'simchöh l'ar-tzay-nu,	בְשִׂמְחָה לְאַרְצֵנוּ,
v'si-tö-aynu big'vulaynu, v'shöm	וְתִטָּעֵנוּ בִּגְבוּלֵנוּ, וְשָׁם
na-aseh l'fönechöh es kör-b'nos	נַעֲשֶׂה לְפָנֶיךָ אֶת קָרְבְּנוֹת
chovosaynu, t'midim k'sidröm	חוֹבוֹתֵינוּ, תְּמִידִים כְּסִדְרָם
umusöfim k'hil'chösöm.	וּמוּסָפִים כְּהִלְכָתָם:
V'es musaf yom ha-shabös	וְאֶת מוּסַף יוֹם הַשַּׁבָּת
ha-zeh, na-aseh v'nak-riv	הַזֶּה, נַעֲשֶׂה וְנַקְרִיב
l'fönechö b'ahavöh, k'mitzvas	לְפָנֶיךָ בְּאַהֲבָה, כְּמִצְוַת
r'tzo-nechö, k'mo she-kösav-tö	רְצוֹנֶךָ, כְּמוֹ שֶׁכָּתַבְתָּ

132

ölaynu b'sorö-sechö, al y'day עָלֵינוּ בְּתוֹרָתֶךָ, עַל יְדֵי

mosheh av-dechö, mipi מֹשֶׁה עַבְדֶּךָ, מִפִּי

ch'vodechö kö-ömur. כְּבוֹדֶךָ כָּאָמוּר:

You have established the Shabbat, desired its offerings, told us the details pertaining to it. Those who delight in it will inherit everlasting glory. May it be Your will, Lord our God and God of our fathers, to bring us up in joy to our land and to plant us within its borders. There we will offer to You the musaf offering of this Shabbat day, in accordance with the command of Your will, as You have prescribed for us in Your Torah, through Moses Your servant in Your glorious Name, as it is stated:

Uv'yom ha-shabös, sh'nay וּבְיוֹם הַשַּׁבָּת, שְׁנֵי

ch'vösim b'nay shönöh כְבָשִׂים בְּנֵי שָׁנָה

t'mimim, ush'nay esronim תְּמִימִם, וּשְׁנֵי עֶשְׂרֹנִים

so-les minchöh b'lulöh סֹלֶת מִנְחָה בְּלוּלָה

va-shemen v'nisko. Olas בַשֶׁמֶן וְנִסְכּוֹ: עֹלַת

sha-bas b'sha-bato, al שַׁבַּת בְּשַׁבַּתּוֹ, עַל

olas ha-tömid v'nisköh. עֹלַת הַתָּמִיד וְנִסְכָּהּ:

On the Shabbat day, two yearling male lambs without blemish, two-tenths [of an ephah] of fine flour mixed with oil as a meal-offering, and its wine-offering — this is the burnt-offering for Shabbat, on each Shabbat, aside from the daily burnt-offering and its wine-offering.

Turn back to page 116, and say from יִשְׂמְחוּ בְמַלְכוּתְךָ **(yism'chu v'mal'chus'chö) through the end of the Amidah.**

Kedusha, for during the repetition of the Amidah. Recited standing, with feet together.

Keser yit'nu l'chö adonöy elohaynu	כֶּתֶר יִתְּנוּ לְךָ יְיָ אֱלֹהֵינוּ
mal-öchim ha-monay ma-löh v'am'chö	מַלְאָכִים הֲמוֹנֵי מַעְלָה וְעַמְּךָ
yisrö-ayl k'vutzay matöh yachad kulöm	יִשְׂרָאֵל קְבוּצֵי מַטָּה, יַחַד כֻּלָּם
k'dushöh l'chö y'sha-layshu ka-kösuv al	קְדֻשָּׁה לְךָ יְשַׁלֵּשׁוּ, כַּכָּתוּב עַל
yad n'vi-echö v'körö zeh el zeh v'ömar.	יַד נְבִיאֶךָ וְקָרָא זֶה אֶל זֶה וְאָמַר:
Ködosh, ködosh, ködosh, adonöy	קָדוֹשׁ, קָדוֹשׁ, קָדוֹשׁ יְיָ
tz'vö-os, m'lo chöl hö-öretz k'vodo.	צְבָאוֹת, מְלֹא כָל הָאָרֶץ כְּבוֹדוֹ:
K'vodo mölay olöm, m'shö-r'söv sho-alim	כְּבוֹדוֹ מָלֵא עוֹלָם, מְשָׁרְתָיו שׁוֹאֲלִים
zeh lözeh, a-yay m'kom k'vodo l'ha-aritzo,	זֶה לָזֶה, אַיֵּה מְקוֹם כְּבוֹדוֹ לְהַעֲרִיצוֹ,
l'umösöm m'shab'chim v'om'rim.	לְעֻמָּתָם מְשַׁבְּחִים וְאוֹמְרִים:
Böruch k'vod adonöy mim'komo.	בָּרוּךְ כְּבוֹד יְיָ מִמְּקוֹמוֹ:
Mim'komo hu yifen b'ra-chamöv l'amo,	מִמְּקוֹמוֹ הוּא יִפֶן בְּרַחֲמָיו לְעַמּוֹ,
ha-m'yachadim sh'mo erev vövoker	הַמְיַחֲדִים שְׁמוֹ עֶרֶב וָבֹקֶר
b'chöl yom tömid, pa-ama-yim	בְּכָל יוֹם תָּמִיד, פַּעֲמַיִם
b'ahavöh sh'ma om'rim.	בְּאַהֲבָה שְׁמַע אוֹמְרִים:
Sh'ma yisrö-ayl adonöy elohaynu adonöy	שְׁמַע יִשְׂרָאֵל יְיָ אֱלֹהֵינוּ
echöd. Hu elohaynu, hu övinu, hu	יְיָ אֶחָד: הוּא אֱלֹהֵינוּ, הוּא אָבִינוּ,
malkaynu, hu moshi-aynu, hu yoshi-aynu	הוּא מַלְכֵּנוּ, הוּא מוֹשִׁיעֵנוּ, הוּא
v'yig-ölaynu shaynis b'körov	יוֹשִׁיעֵנוּ וְיִגְאָלֵנוּ שֵׁנִית בְּקָרוֹב
v'yashmi-aynu b'rachamöv l'aynay köl	וְיַשְׁמִיעֵנוּ בְּרַחֲמָיו לְעֵינֵי כָּל
chai laymor: Hayn gö-alti es'chem acharis	חַי לֵאמֹר: הֵן גָּאַלְתִּי אֶתְכֶם אַחֲרִית

134

kiv'rayshis lih-yos löchem lay-lohim. : כְּבְרֵאשִׁית, לִהְיוֹת לָכֶם לֵאלֹהִים

Ani adonöy elo-haychem. : אֲנִי יְיָ אֱלֹהֵיכֶם

Uv'div'ray köd-sh'chö kösuv laymor. : וּבְדִבְרֵי קָדְשְׁךָ כָּתוּב לֵאמֹר

Yimloch adonöy l'olöm eloha-yich tziyon יִמְלֹךְ יְיָ לְעוֹלָם אֱלֹהַיִךְ צִיּוֹן

l'dor vödor, ha-l'lu-yöh. : לְדֹר וָדֹר, הַלְלוּיָהּ

Modim, for during the repetition of the Amidah. Recited standing. Bow your head while reciting the first five words of Modim.

Modim anach-nu löch, shö-atöh hu מוֹדִים אֲנַחְנוּ לָךְ, שָׁאַתָּה הוּא

adonöy elo-haynu vay-lohay avosaynu, יְיָ אֱלֹהֵינוּ וֵאלֹהֵי אֲבוֹתֵינוּ,

elohay köl bösör, yo-tz'raynu, yo-tzayr אֱלֹהֵי כָּל בָּשָׂר, יוֹצְרֵנוּ, יוֹצֵר

b'rayshis. B'röchos v'hodö-os l'shim'chö בְּרֵאשִׁית, בְּרָכוֹת וְהוֹדָאוֹת לְשִׁמְךָ

ha-gödol v'haködosh, al she-heche-yisönu הַגָּדוֹל וְהַקָּדוֹשׁ, עַל שֶׁהֶחֱיִיתָנוּ

v'kiyam-tönu. kayn t'cha-yaynu וְקִיַּמְתָּנוּ, כֵּן תְּחַיֵּנוּ

us'ka-y'maynu v'se-esof gölu-yosay-nu וּתְקַיְּמֵנוּ, וְתֶאֱסוֹף גָּלֻיּוֹתֵינוּ

l'chatz'ros köd-shechö, v'nöshuv ay-lechö לְחַצְרוֹת קָדְשֶׁךָ, וְנָשׁוּב אֵלֶיךָ

lishmor chukechö, v'la-asos r'tzonechö, לִשְׁמֹר חֻקֶּיךָ, וְלַעֲשׂוֹת רְצוֹנֶךָ,

ul'öv-d'chö b'layvöv shölaym, al she-önu וּלְעָבְדְּךָ בְּלֵבָב שָׁלֵם, עַל שֶׁאָנוּ

modim löch. Böruch ayl ha-hodö-os. : מוֹדִים לָךְ, בָּרוּךְ אֵל הַהוֹדָאוֹת

We thankfully acknowledge that You are the Lord our God and God of our fathers, the God of all flesh, our Creator and the Creator of all existence. We offer blessings and thanks to Your great and holy Name, for You have given us life and sustained us; so may You continue to grant us life and sustain us, gather our dispersed to the courtyards of Your Sanctuary and we shall return to You to keep Your laws, to do Your will, and to serve You with a perfect heart, for we thankfully acknowledge You.

Ayn Kaylokaynu...   **For Levels:** ᗷ ᑕ   אֵין כֵּאלֹהֵינוּ...

Ayn kaylo-haynu, ayn	אֵין כֵּאלֹהֵינוּ, אֵין
kado-naynu, ayn k'malkaynu,	כַּאדוֹנֵינוּ, אֵין כְּמַלְכֵּנוּ,
ayn k'moshi-aynu.	אֵין כְּמוֹשִׁיעֵנוּ:
Mi chaylo-haynu, mi	מִי כֵאלֹהֵינוּ, מִי
chado-naynu, mi ch'malkaynu,	כַאדוֹנֵינוּ, מִי כְמַלְכֵּנוּ,
mi ch'moshi-aynu.	מִי כְמוֹשִׁיעֵנוּ:
Nodeh laylo-haynu, nodeh	נוֹדֶה לֵאלֹהֵינוּ, נוֹדֶה
lado-naynu, nodeh l'malkaynu,	לַאדוֹנֵינוּ, נוֹדֶה לְמַלְכֵּנוּ,
nodeh l'moshi-aynu.	נוֹדֶה לְמוֹשִׁיעֵנוּ:
Böruch elo-haynu, böruch	בָּרוּךְ אֱלֹהֵינוּ, בָּרוּךְ
ado-naynu, böruch malkaynu,	אֲדוֹנֵינוּ, בָּרוּךְ מַלְכֵּנוּ,
böruch moshi-aynu.	בָּרוּךְ מוֹשִׁיעֵנוּ:
Atöh hu elohaynu, atöh	אַתָּה הוּא אֱלֹהֵינוּ, אַתָּה
hu ado-naynu, atöh hu	הוּא אֲדוֹנֵינוּ, אַתָּה הוּא
malkaynu, atöh hu moshi-aynu,	מַלְכֵּנוּ, אַתָּה הוּא מוֹשִׁיעֵנוּ,

atöh soshi-aynu. Atöh sö-kum	אַתָּה תוֹשִׁיעֵנוּ: אַתָּה תָקוּם
t'rachaym tziyon ki ays	תְּרַחֵם צִיּוֹן כִּי עֵת
l'chen'nöh ki vö mo-ayd. Atöh	לְחֶנְנָהּ כִּי בָא מוֹעֵד: אַתָּה
hu adonöy elohaynu vay-lohay	הוּא יְיָ אֱלֹהֵינוּ וֵאלֹהֵי
avo-saynu, she-hiktiru	אֲבוֹתֵינוּ שֶׁהִקְטִירוּ
avosaynu l'fönechö es	אֲבוֹתֵינוּ לְפָנֶיךָ אֶת
k'tores ha-samim.	קְטֹרֶת הַסַּמִּים:

"There is none like our God; there is none like our King; there is none like our Deliverer." This prayer begins the concluding prayers of the morning service. After praying the whole service we proudly and earnestly give voice to the deep feelings of awe and gratitude we have for God.

Ölaynu... **For Levels:** עָלֵינוּ ...
Ⓑ Ⓒ

Ölaynu l'shabay-ach la-adon	עָלֵינוּ לְשַׁבֵּחַ לַאֲדוֹן
ha-kol, lösays g'dulöh l'yo-tzayr	הַכֹּל, לָתֵת גְּדֻלָּה לְיוֹצֵר
b'rayshis, shelo ösönu k'go-yay	בְּרֵאשִׁית, שֶׁלֹּא עָשָׂנוּ כְּגוֹיֵי
hö-arö-tzos, v'lo sömönu	הָאֲרָצוֹת, וְלֹא שָׂמָנוּ
k'mish-p'chos hö-adömöh,	כְּמִשְׁפְּחוֹת הָאֲדָמָה,

137

shelo söm chelkaynu köhem,	שֶׁלֹּא שָׂם חֶלְקֵנוּ כָּהֶם,
v'gorölaynu k'chöl ha-monöm	וְגוֹרָלֵנוּ כְּכָל הֲמוֹנָם
she-haym mishtachavim l'hevel	שֶׁהֵם מִשְׁתַּחֲוִים לְהֶבֶל
v'lörik. Va-anachnu kor'im	וָלָרִיק. וַאֲנַחְנוּ כּוֹרְעִים
umish-tachavim umodim,	וּמִשְׁתַּחֲוִים וּמוֹדִים,
lif'nay melech, mal'chay	לִפְנֵי מֶלֶךְ, מַלְכֵי
ha-m'löchim, ha-ködosh	הַמְּלָכִים, הַקָּדוֹשׁ
böruch hu. She-hu noteh	בָּרוּךְ הוּא. שֶׁהוּא נוֹטֶה
shöma-yim v'yosayd ö-retz,	שָׁמַיִם וְיוֹסֵד אָרֶץ,
umoshav y'köro ba-shöma-yim	וּמוֹשַׁב יְקָרוֹ בַּשָּׁמַיִם
mima-al, ush'chinas uzo	מִמַּעַל, וּשְׁכִינַת עֻזּוֹ
b'göv'hay m'romim, hu	בְּגָבְהֵי מְרוֹמִים, הוּא
elohaynu ayn od. Emes	אֱלֹהֵינוּ אֵין עוֹד. אֱמֶת
malkaynu, efes zulöso,	מַלְכֵּנוּ, אֶפֶס זוּלָתוֹ,
kakösuv b'soröso: V'yöda-tö	כַּכָּתוּב בְּתוֹרָתוֹ: וְיָדַעְתָּ
ha-yom va-hashay-vosö el	הַיּוֹם וַהֲשֵׁבֹתָ אֶל
l'vövechö, ki adonöy hu	לְבָבֶךָ, כִּי יְיָ הוּא
hö-elohim ba-shöma-yim	הָאֱלֹהִים בַּשָּׁמַיִם

mima-al, v'al hö-öretz   מִמַּעַל, וְעַל הָאָרֶץ

mi-töchas, ayn od.   מִתָּחַת, אֵין עוֹד:

This is a very, very old prayer. The famous Rav Hai Gaon, the last of the Babylonian Geonim, states that this prayer was composed by Joshua, as he led the children of Israel into the Promised Land. (The initials of the first sentences, read backwards, form his original name "Hoshea.") Thus, when Joshua was about to settle the Jewish people in the Holy Land, he made them remember, through this prayer, that they were different from the other nations and tribes of the earth. It is a very important prayer, and everyone should be familiar with it. Jewish Law requires that when it is recited in the synagogue, everyone join in it, even if one has already said it, or just happened to walk into the synagogue at that time.

V'al kayn n'ka-veh l'chö   וְעַל כֵּן נְקַוֶּה לְּךָ

adonöy elohaynu, lir-os   יְיָ אֱלֹהֵינוּ, לִרְאוֹת

m'hayröh b'sif-eres uzechö,   מְהֵרָה בְּתִפְאֶרֶת עֻזֶּךָ,

l'ha-avir gilulim min hö-öretz   לְהַעֲבִיר גִּלּוּלִים מִן הָאָרֶץ

v'hö-elilim köros yiköray-sun,   וְהָאֱלִילִים כָּרוֹת יִכָּרֵתוּן,

l'sakayn olöm b'mal'chus   לְתַקֵּן עוֹלָם בְּמַלְכוּת

shadai, v'chöl b'nay vösör yik-r'u   שַׁדַּי, וְכָל בְּנֵי בָשָׂר

vish'mechö, l'hafnos ay-lechö köl   יִקְרְאוּ בִשְׁמֶךָ, לְהַפְנוֹת

rish'ay öretz. Yakiru   אֵלֶיךָ כָּל רִשְׁעֵי אָרֶץ. יַכִּירוּ

v'yay-d'u köl yosh'vay sayvayl, ki   וְיֵדְעוּ כָּל יוֹשְׁבֵי תֵבֵל, כִּי

l'chö tichra köl berech, tishöva	לְךָ תִּכְרַע כָּל בֶּרֶךְ, תִּשָּׁבַע
köl löshon. L'fönechö adonöy	כָּל לָשׁוֹן. לְפָנֶיךָ יְיָ
elohaynu yich-r'u v'yipolu,	אֱלֹהֵינוּ יִכְרְעוּ וְיִפּוֹלוּ,
v'lich'vod shim'chö y'kör yitaynu,	וְלִכְבוֹד שִׁמְךָ יְקָר יִתֵּנוּ,
vi-kab'lu chulöm alay-hem es	וִיקַבְּלוּ כֻלָּם עֲלֵיהֶם אֶת
ol mal'chusechö, v'simloch	עוֹל מַלְכוּתֶךָ, וְתִמְלֹךְ
alayhem m'hayröh l'olöm vö-ed,	עֲלֵיהֶם מְהֵרָה לְעוֹלָם וָעֶד,
ki ha-mal'chus shel'chö hi,	כִּי הַמַּלְכוּת שֶׁלְּךָ הִיא,
ul'ol'may ad tim-loch	וּלְעוֹלְמֵי עַד תִּמְלֹךְ
b'chövod, ka-kösuv	בְּכָבוֹד, כַּכָּתוּב
b'sörösechö, adonöy yimloch	בְּתוֹרָתֶךָ: יְיָ יִמְלֹךְ
l'olöm vö-ed. V'ne-emar,	לְעֹלָם וָעֶד. וְנֶאֱמַר:
v'hö-yöh adonöy l'melech al köl	וְהָיָה יְיָ לְמֶלֶךְ עַל
hö-öretz, ba-yom	כָּל הָאָרֶץ, בַּיּוֹם
hahu yih-yeh adonöy	הַהוּא יִהְיֶה יְיָ
echöd ush'mo echöd.	אֶחָד וּשְׁמוֹ אֶחָד:

In this prayer we express our hope for that Great Day when all the people of the earth will recognize God.

140

Al tirö mipachad pis-om,	אַל תִּירָא מִפַּחַד פִּתְאֹם,
umisho-as r'shö-im ki sövo.	וּמִשֹּׁאַת רְשָׁעִים כִּי תָבֹא :
Utzu ay-tzöh v'suför, dab'ru	עֻצוּ עֵצָה וְתֻפָר, דַּבְּרוּ
dövör v'lo yökum, ki imönu	דָבָר וְלֹא יָקוּם, כִּי עִמָּנוּ
ayl. V'ad zik-nöh ani hu,	אֵל : וְעַד זִקְנָה אֲנִי הוּא,
v'ad sayvöh ani esbol, ani	וְעַד שֵׂיבָה אֲנִי אֶסְבֹּל, אֲנִי
ösisi va-ani esö, va-ani	עָשִׂיתִי וַאֲנִי אֶשָּׂא, וַאֲנִי
esbol va-amalayt. Ach tzadikim	אֶסְבֹּל וַאֲמַלֵּט : אַךְ צַדִּיקִים
yodu lish'mechö yay-sh'vu	יוֹדוּ לִשְׁמֶךָ יֵשְׁבוּ
y'shörim es pönechö.	יְשָׁרִים אֶת פָּנֶיךָ :

These meaningful verses express an important message to us as we conclude the service and are about to part ways. They remind us that no matter how long our exile may be, or what fears and anxieties beset us, God will always 'carry' us. We are God's responsibility. He will surely deliver us from our enemies and from the exile.

Psalm 20

For Levels:

Ⓑ Ⓒ

תְּהִלִּים - פֶּרֶק כ׳

It is a great custom to recite Tehilim (Psalms) every day. The book of Tehilim was composed by King David. He ruled the Jewish people during the times of the Holy Temple which stood in Jerusalem some 2,000 years ago. His psalms open the heart and express the collective thoughts and emotions of the Jewish people. We have included chapter 20, which is a very fitting psalm to say whenever in need.

Lam'na-tzay-ach mizmor	לַמְנַצֵּחַ מִזְמוֹר
l'dövid. Ya-an'chö adonöy	לְדָוִד: יַעַנְךָ יְיָ
b'yom tzörö, y'sagev'chö	בְּיוֹם צָרָה, יְשַׂגֶּבְךָ שֵׁם
shaym elohay ya-akov. Yishlach	אֱלֹהֵי יַעֲקֹב: יִשְׁלַח
ez-r'chö mikodesh, umi-tziyon	עֶזְרְךָ מִקֹּדֶשׁ, וּמִצִּיּוֹן
yis-ödekö. Yizkor köl	יִסְעָדֶךָ: יִזְכֹּר כָּל
min'chosechö, v'olös'chö	מִנְחֹתֶיךָ, וְעוֹלָתְךָ
y'dash'neh selöh. Yiten l'chö	יְדַשְּׁנֶה סֶלָה: יִתֶּן לְךָ
chil'vö-vechö, v'chöl atzös'chö	כִלְבָבֶךָ, וְכָל עֲצָתְךָ
y'ma-lay. N'ran'nöh	יְמַלֵּא: נְרַנְּנָה
bishu-ösechö, uv'shaym	בִּישׁוּעָתֶךָ, וּבְשֵׁם

142

elohaynu nidgol, y'malay	אֱלֹהֵינוּ נִדְגֹּל, יְמַלֵּא
adonöy köl mish-alosechö.	יְיָ כָּל מִשְׁאֲלוֹתֶיךָ :
Atöh yöda-ti, ki hoshi-a adonöy	עַתָּה יָדַעְתִּי, כִּי הוֹשִׁיעַ יְיָ
m'shicho, ya-anayhu mish'mey	מְשִׁיחוֹ, יַעֲנֵהוּ מִשְּׁמֵי
köd-sho, big'vuros yay-sha	קָדְשׁוֹ, בִּגְבוּרוֹת יֵשַׁע
y'mino. Ayleh vö-rechev, v'ayleh	יְמִינוֹ: אֵלֶּה בָרֶכֶב, וְאֵלֶּה
va-susim, va-anachnu b'shaym	בַסּוּסִים, וַאֲנַחְנוּ בְּשֵׁם
adonöy elohaynu nazkir.	יְיָ אֱלֹהֵינוּ נַזְכִּיר :
Haymöh kör'u v'növölu,	הֵמָּה כָּרְעוּ וְנָפָלוּ,
va-anachnu kam-nu vanis-odöd.	וַאֲנַחְנוּ קַמְנוּ וַנִּתְעוֹדָד :
Adonöy ho-shiöh, ha-melech	יְיָ הוֹשִׁיעָה, הַמֶּלֶךְ
ya-anaynu v'yom kör'aynu.	יַעֲנֵנוּ בְיוֹם קָרְאֵנוּ :

For the Choirmaster; a Psalm by David. May the Lord answer you on the day of distress; may the Name of the God of Jacob fortify you. May He send your help from the Sanctuary, and support you from Zion. May He remember all your offerings, and always accept favorably your sacrifices. May He grant you your heart's desire, and fulfill your every counsel. We will rejoice in your deliverance, and raise our banners in the name of our God; may the Lord fulfill all your wishes. Now I know that the Lord has delivered His anointed one, answering him from His holy heavens with the mighty saving power of His right hand. Some (rely) upon chariots and some upon horses, but we [rely upon and] invoke the Name of the Lord our God. They bend and fall, but we rise and stand firm. Lord, deliver us; may the King answer us on the day we call.

The 12 Pesukim — **For Levels:** Ⓐ Ⓑ Ⓒ — י״ב פְּסוּקִים

It is a positive Mitzvah for every Jew, boy or girl, man or woman, to learn Torah each and every day. Here are selected verses drawn from the Torah and contains its deepest truths. Recite them each day, or even better, study them by heart!

1. Toröh tzivöh lönu moshe, **1. תּוֹרָה צִוָּה לָנוּ מֹשֶׁה**
moröshöh k'hilas ya-akov. **מוֹרָשָׁה קְהִלַּת יַעֲקֹב:**

The Torah that Moshe commanded us is the heritage of the congregation of Yaakov. (Deut. 33:4)

2. Sh'ma yisrö-ayl adonöy **2. שְׁמַע יִשְׂרָאֵל יְיָ**
elohaynu adonöy echöd. **אֱלֹהֵינוּ יְיָ אֶחָד:**

"Hear O Israel, G-d is our Lord, G-d is One." (Deut. 6:4)

3. B'chöl dor vödor cha-yöv **3. בְּכָל דּוֹר וָדוֹר חַיָּב**
ödöm lir-os es atzmo **אָדָם לִרְאוֹת אֶת עַצְמוֹ**
k'ilu hu yö-tzö mimitzrö-yim. **כְּאִלּוּ הוּא יָצָא מִמִּצְרָיִם:**

In every generation one must look upon himself as if he personally had gone out of Egypt! (Talmud, Pesachim 116b)

4. Köl yisrö-ayl yaysh löhem
chaylek l'olöm haböh,
she-ne-emar, v'amaych kulöm
tzadikim l'olöm yi-r'shu öretz,
naytzer ma-tö-ai ma-asay
yödai l'hispö-ayr.

4. כָּל יִשְׂרָאֵל יֵשׁ לָהֶם
חֵלֶק לְעוֹלָם הַבָּא,
שֶׁנֶּאֱמַר, וְעַמֵּךְ כֻּלָּם
צַדִּיקִים לְעוֹלָם יִירְשׁוּ אָרֶץ,
נֵצֶר מַטָּעַי מַעֲשֵׂה
יָדַי לְהִתְפָּאֵר:

All Israel have a share in the World To Come, as it is stated (Isaiah 60:21):
'And your people are all tzadikim (righteous). They shall inherit the land
forever. They are the branch of My planting, the work of My hands, in which
I take pride.' (Talmud, Sanhedrin 90a)

5. Ki körov aylechö
ha-dövör m'od b'fichö
uvil'vöv'chö la-a-soso.

5. כִּי קָרוֹב אֵלֶיךָ
הַדָּבָר מְאֹד בְּפִיךָ
וּבִלְבָבְךָ לַעֲשׂוֹתוֹ:

It is within your close reach to follow the Torah in speech, feeling and deed.
(Deut. 30:14, as explained in Tanya)

6. V'hinay hashem nitzöv ölöv
um'lo chöl hö-öretz k'vodo
umabit ölöv uvochayn k'lö-yos
vö-layv, im ov'do körö-uy.

6. וְהִנֵּה ה' נִצָּב עָלָיו
וּמְלֹא כָל הָאָרֶץ כְּבוֹדוֹ
וּמַבִּיט עָלָיו וּבוֹחֵן כְּלָיוֹת
וָלֵב, אִם עוֹבְדוֹ כָּרָאוּי:

145

G-d stands over him, and the whole earth is full of His glory, and He searches his mind and heart, if he is serving Him as is fitting. (Tanya, Chapter 41)

7. B'rayshis börö elohim ays ha-shöma-yim v'ays hö-öretz.

בְּרֵאשִׁית בָּרָא אֱלֹהִים אֵת הַשָּׁמַיִם וְאֵת הָאָרֶץ:

In the beginning G-d created the heavens and the earth. (Genesis 1:1)

8. V'shinan-töm l'vö-nechö v'dibartö böm, b'shiv-t'chö b'vaysechö, uv'lech-t'chö vaderech, uv'shöch-b'chö, uv'kumechö.

וְשִׁנַּנְתָּם לְבָנֶיךָ וְדִבַּרְתָּ בָּם בְּשִׁבְתְּךָ בְּבֵיתֶךָ וּבְלֶכְתְּךָ בַדֶּרֶךְ וּבְשָׁכְבְּךָ וּבְקוּמֶךָ:

And you shall teach the Torah to your children, and you should speak about it when you are home and when you travel, before you lie down to sleep and when you wake up. (Deut. 6:7)

9. Yöga-ti v'lo mö-tzösi al ta-amin, lo yöga-ti umö-tzösi al ta-amin, yöga-ti umö-tzösi, ta-amin.

יָגַעְתִּי וְלֹא מָצָאתִי אַל תַּאֲמִין, לֹא יָגַעְתִּי וּמָצָאתִי אַל תַּאֲמִין, יָגַעְתִּי וּמָצָאתִי תַּאֲמִין:

If someone says, "I have worked hard, and I have not been successful," don't believe him. If someone says, "I have not worked hard and I have been

successful," don't believe him. If someone says, "I have worked hard and I have been successful," believe him! (Talmud, Megilla, 6b)

10. V'öhav-tö l'ray-achö kömochö,   ,וְאָהַבְתָּ לְרֵעֲךָ כָּמוֹךָ

rabi akivö omayr, zeh   רַבִּי עֲקִיבָא אוֹמֵר, זֶה

k'lal gödol ba-toröh.   : כְּלָל גָּדוֹל בַּתּוֹרָה

Rabbi Akiva says that, "To love your fellow as yourself," is a great basic principle of the Torah. (Leviticus 19:18, Midrash)

12. V'zeh köl hö-ödöm   11. וְזֶה כָּל הָאָדָם

v'sachlis b'ri-öso uv'ri-as   וְתַכְלִית בְּרִיאָתוֹ וּבְרִיאַת

köl hö-olömos, elyonim   כָּל הָעוֹלָמוֹת, עֶלְיוֹנִים

v'sach-tonim, lih-yos lo   וְתַחְתּוֹנִים, לִהְיוֹת לוֹ

dirö zo b'sach-tonim.   : דִּירָה זוֹ בַּתַּחְתּוֹנִים

The purpose of the creation of every Jew and of all the worlds is to make a dwelling place for G-d in this world. (Tanya, Chapter 33)

12. Yismach yisrö-ayl b'osöv,   ,יִשְׂמַח יִשְׂרָאֵל בְּעוֹשָׂיו .12

payrush she-köl mi she-hu   פֵּירוּשׁ שֶׁכָּל מִי שֶׁהוּא

mi-zera yisrö-ayl yaysh lo   מִזֶּרַע יִשְׂרָאֵל יֵשׁ לוֹ

lismo-ach b'simchas hashem,   ,לִשְׂמוֹחַ בְּשִׂמְחַת ה'

asher sös v'sömay-ach　אֲשֶׁר שָׂשׂ וְשָׂמֵחַ

b'diröso b'sachtonim.　בְּדִירָתוֹ בְּתַחְתּוֹנִים :

The Jews should rejoice in their maker. Every Jew should share in G-d's joy, Who rejoices and is happy in His dwelling in this world. (Tanya, chapter 33)

Various Blessings　　**For Levels:**　　בִּרְכוֹת הַנֶּהֱנִין

𝓐 𝓑 𝓒

For thousands of years Jewish people have made blessings before and after eating food. It is how we say 'thank you' to God for all that He has provides us. It also reminds us that eating is not simply a physical activity but an opportunity to use the new energy to do more Mitzvot and perform more acts of kindness.

Blessing For Bread and Bread Products

Before eating bread we must wash our hands ritually. Remove any rings. Fill a large cup with at least 3.5 ounces of cold water, while holding it in your right hand. Transfer the cup to your left hand and pour three times over your whole right hand. Transfer it to your right hand and pour three times over your whole left hand. Rub your hands together and recite the blessing below. After you have finished eating bread, a special, longer "Grace After Meals" is recited (see regular Siddur, prayer book.)

Böruch atöh adonöy, elohaynu	בָּרוּךְ אַתָּה יְיָ, אֱלֹהֵינוּ
melech hö-olöm, asher	מֶלֶךְ הָעוֹלָם, אֲשֶׁר
kid'shönu b'mitzvosöv,	קִדְּשָׁנוּ בְּמִצְוֹתָיו,
v'tzivönu al n'tilas yödö-yim.	וְצִוָּנוּ עַל נְטִילַת יָדָיִם:

Blessed are You, Lord our God, King of the universe, who has sanctified us with His commandments, and commanded us concerning the washing of the hands.

Dry your hands and do not talk until you have made the following blessing and have eaten a piece of bread.

Böruch atöh adonöy,	בָּרוּךְ אַתָּה יְיָ,
elohaynu melech hö-olöm,	אֱלֹהֵינוּ מֶלֶךְ הָעוֹלָם,
hamo-tzi lechem min hö-öretz.	הַמּוֹצִיא לֶחֶם מִן הָאָרֶץ:

Blessed are You, Lord our God, King of the universe, who brings forth bread from the earth.

Blessing For Cookies, Crackers, Wafers, etc.

Böruch atöh adonöy,	בָּרוּךְ אַתָּה יְיָ,
elohaynu melech hö-olöm,	אֱלֹהֵינוּ מֶלֶךְ הָעוֹלָם,
boray minay m'zonos.	בּוֹרֵא מִינֵי מְזוֹנוֹת:

Blessed are You, Lord our God, King of the universe, who creates various kinds of food.

Blessing For All Drinks (except from grapes), Meat, Fish, Milk, Eggs and Cheese

Böruch atöh adonöy, בָּרוּךְ אַתָּה יְיָ,

elohaynu melech hö-olöm, אֱלֹהֵינוּ מֶלֶךְ הָעוֹלָם,

she-hakol nih-yöh bid'vöro. שֶׁהַכֹּל נִהְיָה בִּדְבָרוֹ:

Blessed are You, Lord our God, King of the universe, by whose word all things came to be.

Blessing For Wine or Grape Juice

Böruch atöh adonöy בָּרוּךְ אַתָּה יְיָ,

elohaynu melech hö-olöm, אֱלֹהֵינוּ מֶלֶךְ הָעוֹלָם,

boray p'ri ha-göfen. בּוֹרֵא פְּרִי הַגָּפֶן:

Blessed are You, Lord our God, King of the universe, who creates the fruit of the vine.

Blessing For All Tree-Grown Fruits

Böruch atöh adonöy בָּרוּךְ אַתָּה יְיָ,

elohaynu melech hö-olöm, אֱלֹהֵינוּ מֶלֶךְ הָעוֹלָם,

boray p'ri hö-aytz. בּוֹרֵא פְּרִי הָעֵץ:

Blessed are You, Lord our God, King of the universe, who creates the fruit of the tree.

Blessing For All Vegetables (Earth-Grown Fruits)

Böruch atöh adonöy,   בָּרוּךְ אַתָּה יְיָ,

elohaynu melech hö-olöm,   אֱלֹהֵינוּ מֶלֶךְ הָעוֹלָם,

boray p'ri hö-adömöh.   בּוֹרֵא פְּרִי הָאֲדָמָה:

Blessed are You, Lord our God, King of the universe, who creates the fruit of the earth.

Blessing When Smelling Sweet Aromatic Spices

Böruch atöh adonöy,   בָּרוּךְ אַתָּה יְיָ,

elohaynu melech hö-olöm,   אֱלֹהֵינוּ מֶלֶךְ הָעוֹלָם,

boray minay v'sömim.   בּוֹרֵא מִינֵי בְשָׂמִים:

Blessed are You, Lord our God, King of the universe, who creates various kinds of spices.

Blessing When Hearing a Thunder

Böruch atöh adonöy,   בָּרוּךְ אַתָּה יְיָ,

elohaynu melech hö-olöm,   אֱלֹהֵינוּ מֶלֶךְ הָעוֹלָם,

shekocho ug'vuröso   שֶׁכֹּחוֹ וּגְבוּרָתוֹ

mölay olöm.   מָלֵא עוֹלָם:

Blessed are You, Lord our God, King of the universe, whose power and might fill the world.

Blessing When Seeing a Lightning

Böruch atöh adonöy,   בָּרוּךְ אַתָּה יְיָ,

elohaynu melech hö-olöm,   אֱלֹהֵינוּ מֶלֶךְ הָעוֹלָם,

osay ma-asay v'rayshis.   עוֹשֶׂה מַעֲשֵׂה בְרֵאשִׁית:

Blessed are You, Lord our God, King of the universe, who re-enacts the work of Creation.

Blessings For After Eating

Blessing After a Meal with Bread

Abbreviated for young children. For full Grace, see regular Siddur.

B'rich racha-mönö, elö-hönö,   בְּרִיךְ רַחֲמָנָא, אֱלָהָנָא,

mal-kö d'öl'mö,   מַלְכָּא דְעָלְמָא,

mörö d'hai pitö.   מָרָא דְהַאי פִּיתָּא:

Blessed is the Lord our God, King of the universe, Master of this bread.

Blessing After a Snack or Wine

The following is said after eating at least 1 ounce of cooked or baked food prepared from the five species of grain [wheat, barley, rye, oats or

spelt], and after eating wine, grapes, figs, pomegranates, olives or dates. If one ate any of these fruits, and also ate cake and/or drank wine (or grape juice), he should combine the items together in the blessing. For other foods and drinks (except bread), recite *Boray N'föshos* (page 157).

Böruch atöh adonöy, elohaynu
melech hö-olöm

בָּרוּךְ אַתָּה יְיָ, אֱלֹהֵינוּ
מֶלֶךְ הָעוֹלָם

After foods prepared from the five grains: עַל ה׳ מִינֵי דָגָן :
al ha-mich-yöh v'al ha-kalkölöh

עַל הַמִּחְיָה וְעַל הַכַּלְכָּלָה

After wine: עַל הַיַּיִן :
(v')al ha-gefen v'al p'ri ha-gefen

(וְ)עַל הַגֶּפֶן וְעַל פְּרִי הַגֶּפֶן

**After grapes, figs, pomegranates,
olives or dates:**
עַל פֵּירוֹת
מִז׳ מִינִים :
(v')al hö-aytz v'al p'ri hö-aytz

(וְ)עַל הָעֵץ וְעַל פְּרִי הָעֵץ

v'al t'nuvas ha-sö-deh v'al eretz
chemdöh tovöh ur'chövöh
sherö-tzisö v'hin-chaltö
la-avosaynu le-echol mipir-yöh
v'lisbo-a mi-tuvöh, rachem nö

וְעַל תְּנוּבַת הַשָּׂדֶה וְעַל אֶרֶץ
חֶמְדָּה טוֹבָה וּרְחָבָה
שֶׁרָצִיתָ וְהִנְחַלְתָּ
לַאֲבוֹתֵינוּ לֶאֱכוֹל מִפִּרְיָהּ
וְלִשְׂבּוֹעַ מִטּוּבָהּ, רַחֵם נָא

153

adonöy elohaynu al yisrö-ayl	יְיָ אֱלֹהֵינוּ עַל יִשְׂרָאֵל
amechö v'al y'rushöla-yim	עַמֶּךָ וְעַל יְרוּשָׁלַיִם
irechö v'al tziyon mishkan	עִירֶךָ וְעַל צִיּוֹן מִשְׁכַּן
k'vodechö v'al miz-b'chechö	כְּבוֹדֶךָ וְעַל מִזְבְּחֶךָ
v'al hay-chölechö uv'nay	וְעַל הֵיכָלֶךָ וּבְנֵה
y'rushöla-yim ir ha-kodesh	יְרוּשָׁלַיִם עִיר הַקֹּדֶשׁ
bim'hayröh v'yömaynu	בִּמְהֵרָה בְיָמֵינוּ
v'ha-alaynu l'sochöh,	וְהַעֲלֵנוּ לְתוֹכָהּ,
v'sam'chaynu vöh un'vörech'chö	וְשַׂמְּחֵנוּ בָהּ וּנְבָרֶכְךָ
bi'kdushö uv'töhöröh,	בִּקְדֻשָּׁה וּבְטָהֳרָה,

On Shabbat: בשבת:

ur'tzay v'hachali-tzaynu b'yom	וּרְצֵה וְהַחֲלִיצֵנוּ בְּיוֹם
ha-shabös ha-zeh,	הַשַּׁבָּת הַזֶּה,

On Rosh Chodesh, Festivals, בר״ח ויו״ט
and Chol HaMoed: ובחוה״מ:

v'zöch'raynu l'tovöh b'yom	וְזָכְרֵנוּ לְטוֹבָה בְּיוֹם

On Rosh Chodesh: בר״ח:

rosh ha-chodesh ha-zeh,	רֹאשׁ הַחֹדֶשׁ הַזֶּה,

On Rosh Hashana: בראש השנה:

ha-ziköron ha-zeh, הַזִּכָּרוֹן הַזֶּה,

On Pesach: בפסח:

chag ha-matzos ha-zeh, חַג הַמַּצּוֹת הַזֶּה,

On Shavuot: בשבועות:

chag ha-shövu-os ha-zeh, חַג הַשָּׁבֻעוֹת הַזֶּה,

On Sukkot: בסוכות:

chag ha-sukkos ha-zeh, חַג הַסֻּכּוֹת הַזֶּה,

On Shmini Atzeret and Simchat Torah: בשמ"ע ושמח"ת:

sh'mini atzeres ha-chag ha-zeh שְׁמִינִי עֲצֶרֶת הֶחָג הַזֶּה

Ki atöh adonöy tov umaytiv כִּי אַתָּה יְיָ טוֹב וּמֵטִיב

la-kol v'no-deh l'chö al hö-öretz לַכֹּל וְנוֹדֶה לְךָ עַל הָאָרֶץ

After foods prepared from the five grains: על ה' מיני דגן:

v'al ha-mich-yöh. וְעַל הַמִּחְיָה.

After wine: על היין:

v'al p'ri ha-göfen. וְעַל פְּרִי הַגָּפֶן.

155

After grapes, figs,
pomegranates, olives or dates:

על פירות
מז׳ מינים:

v'al ha-payros.

וְעַל הַפֵּרוֹת.

Böruch atöh adonöy, al
hö-öretz

בָּרוּךְ אַתָּה יְיָ, עַל
הָאָרֶץ

After foods prepared from the five grains:

על ה׳ מיני דגן:

v'al ha-mich-yöh.

וְעַל הַמִּחְיָה:

After wine:

על היין:

v'al p'ri ha-göfen.

וְעַל פְּרִי הַגָּפֶן:

After grapes, figs,
pomegranates, olives or dates:

על פירות
מז׳ מינים:

v'al ha-payros.

וְעַל הַפֵּרוֹת:

Blessed are You, Lord our God, King of the universe, for: *After prepared foods from the five kinds of grain:* the sustenance and the nourishment. *After wine:* the vine and the fruit of the vine. *After grapes, figs pomegranates, olives or dates:* the tree and the fruit of the tree, for the produce of the field, and for the precious, good and spacious land which You have graciously given as a heritage to our ancestors, to eat of its fruit and be satiated with its goodness. Have mercy, Lord our God, on Israel Your people, on Jerusalem Your city, on Zion the abode of Your glory, on Your altar and on Your Temple. Rebuild Jerusalem, the holy city, speedily in our days, and bring us up to it and make us rejoice in it, and we will bless You in holiness and purity. (*On Shabbat:* May it please You to strengthen us on this Shabbat day.) *On Rosh Chodesh, Festivals and Chol HaMoed:* Remember us for good on this

day of: (*on Rosh Chodesh*: Rosh Chodesh). (*On Rosh Hashana*: Remembrance). (*On Pesach*: the Festival of Matzot). (*On Shavuot*: the Festival of Shavuot). (*On Sukkot*: the Festival of Sukkot). (*On Shmini Atzeret & Simchat Torah*: Shmini Atzeret, the Festival). For You, Lord, are good and do good to all, and we offer thanks to You for the land and for: *After food prepared from the five kinds of grain*: the sustenance. *After wine*: (and) the fruit of the vine. *After grapes, figs pomegranates, olives or dates*: (and) the fruits. Blessed are You Lord, for the land, *After food prepared from the five kinds of grain*: and for the sustenance. *After wine*: and for the fruit of the vine, *After grapes, figs, pomegranates, olives or dates*: and for the fruits.

Blessing After Other Snacks or Drinks

The following blessing is recited after any foods or drink upon which Grace After Meals or Grace After a Snack does not apply (i,e, eggs, cheese, chocolates, candies, ice cream, most drinks (except wine or grape juice)).

Böruch atöh adonöy,	בָּרוּךְ אַתָּה יְיָ,
elohaynu melech hö-olöm,	אֱלֹהֵינוּ מֶלֶךְ הָעוֹלָם,
boray n'föshos rabos	בּוֹרֵא נְפָשׁוֹת רַבּוֹת
v'chesronön al kol mah	וְחֶסְרוֹנָן עַל כֹּל מַה
shebörösö l'hacha-yos bö-hem	שֶׁבָּרֵאתָ לְהַחֲיוֹת בָּהֶם
nefesh köl chöy. Böruch	נֶפֶשׁ כָּל חָי. בָּרוּךְ
chay hö-olömim.	חֵי הָעוֹלָמִים:

Blessed are You, Lord our God, King of the universe, Creator of numerous living beings and their needs, for all the things You have created with which to sustain the soul of every living being, Blessed is He who is the Life of the worlds.

Tzör'chai Amchö...   **For Levels:**   ...צָרְכֵי עַמְּךָ
                          Ⓐ

The following prayer is for toddlers and very young children who cannot yet recite the entire Amidah.

Tzör'chay am'chö yisrö-ayl	צָרְכֵי עַמְּךָ יִשְׂרָאֵל
m'rubim v'da-töm k'tzöröh.	מְרֻבִּים וְדַעְתָּם קְצָרָה:
Y'hi rö-tzon mil'fönechö,	יְהִי רָצוֹן מִלְּפָנֶיךָ,
adonöy elohaynu, she-titayn	יְיָ אֱלֹהֵינוּ, שֶׁתִּתֶּן
l'chöl echöd v'echöd k'day	לְכָל אֶחָד וְאֶחָד כְּדֵי
far-nösöso, ul'chöl g'viyöh	פַּרְנָסָתוֹ, וּלְכָל גְּוִיָּה
ug'vi-yöh day mach-soröh,	וּגְוִיָּה דֵי מַחְסוֹרָהּ,
v'ha-tov b'ay-nechö asay.	וְהַטּוֹב בְּעֵינֶיךָ עֲשֵׂה.
Böruch atöh adonöy,	בָּרוּךְ אַתָּה יְיָ,
shomay-a t'filöh.	שׁוֹמֵעַ תְּפִלָּה:

The needs of Your nation Israel are many and they don't know how to request all their needs. May it be Your will, Lord our God, that you give each and everyone adequate sustenance, and fill everybody's wants, and do that which You deem proper. Blessed are You God, who accepts prayer.

Our Other Books

The Shabbat Table Companion: Transliterated *Kiddush*, *Bencher*, and Songs
Easy-to-read English transliterations, concise explanations, plus over 140 popular Shabbat and Yom Tov table songs to help create a true Shabbat atmosphere in your home. *Softcover; 6.5x5.5; 160 pages; JLG-01; ISBN 1-891293-11-7; $8.95 (Audio edition available)*

The Shabbat Synagogue Companion: Explains Prayers for Shabbat Eve and Shabbat Day
A complete guide to the prayer services of both Friday evening and Shabbat morning. It maps every prayer and explains their origin and meaning. It includes English transliterations of many key prayers and instructions for common synagogue honors such as opening the Ark or being called to the Torah. *Softcover; 6.5x5.5; 160 pages; JLG-02; ISBN 1-891293-12-5; $8.95 (Audio edition available)*

The *Kabbalat Shabbat* Synagogue Companion: Transliterations and Explanations
Includes the complete Friday evening service, along with easy-to-read English transliterations, clear instructions, and a concise overview of Shabbat and prayer. This plain language guide will enable you to pray, sing along, and comprehend the services at a higher level. *Softcover; 6.5x5.5; 160 pages; JLG-04; ISBN 1-891293-14-1; $8.95 (Audio edition available)*

The High Holiday Synagogue Companion: Transliterations and Explanations
A page-by-page guide through the Chabad Hebrew/English edition of the Rosh Hashanah and Yom Kippur prayerbook, explaining what prayers are found on each page, their origin, meaning, and the proper action required at each point. Includes key prayers and many inspirational readings and stories. *Softcover; JLG-03; ISBN 1-891293-10-9; $8.95*

The Passover Seder Table Companion: Transliterations and Explanations
The entire Hagaddah transliterated! Guides you step-by-step through the Passover Seder and all its preparations. Includes a clear and concise overview of Passover, easy-to-read English transliterations, clear instruction, plus a collection of over 50 popular holiday table songs. *Softcover; 6.5x5.5; 160 pages; JLG-06; ISBN 1-891293-17-6; $8.95*

The Complete Jewish Wedding Companion: Guide to a Traditional Jewish Wedding
The ultimate guide to understanding and enjoying a traditional Jewish wedding experience. The Jewish Wedding Companion takes you through all the steps with clear instructions, explanations, and directions. Includes all relevant prayers, liturgy, and blessings. *Softcover; 6.5x5.5; 128 pages; JLG-07; ISBN 1-891293-18-4; $8.95 (bulk discounts available)*

לזכות: יוסף בן חי׳ מלכה, חנה פריווא בת אלטער יהושוע הכהן, הירשל פסח בן דוד, רייזא פייגא בת דוד, שניאור זלמן בן חנה
פריווא, דבורה גבריאלה בת רייזא פייגא, מנחם מענדל בן מרים שרה, מניא שיינא בת מרים שרה, חנה פריווא בת דבורה גבריאלה

the
jewish
LEARNING GROUP

OUR MISSION
To assist Jewish people on their path
to joyful Jewish observance.

WHAT WE DO
We create plain language how-to guides
on Jewish law and custom, traditioal prayer
texts with transliteration and instruction,
and educational audio and video guides.
Our innovative products help people attain
the rudimentary knowledge and confidence
needed to build, lead, and further their
Jewish observance at a comfortable and
gradual pace.

Wer'e Here for You!

See our entire catalog online at
www.JewishLearningGroup.com
or call 1-888-56-LEARN